About the author

Gemma Bray started The Organised Mum Method in 2006 when her first child was born. Fed up with the housework getting out of control, she devised a cleaning routine and stuck it on the fridge. TOMM was born. In January 2017, Gemma put it all down in a blog and shared TOMM with readers. The response was a phenomenon, with TOMM devotees crediting the method with transforming their home life.

The Organised Mum Method showed you how to master the housework to stop it taking over your life. Now Gemma has devised The Organised Time Technique, a method for taking control of the rest of your day – and the rest of your life – so that you can spend your time on the things that are most important to you.

the Organised Time Technique

How to Get Your Life Running Like Clockwork

GEMMA BRAY

PIATKUS

PIATKUS

First published in Great Britain in 2020 by Piatkus

1 3 5 7 9 10 8 6 4 2

Copyright © Gemma Bray 2020

The moral right of the author has been asserted.

A CIP catalogue record for this book
is available from the British Library.

ISBN 978-0-349-42697-6

Typeset in Sabon by M Rules
Printed and bound in Great Britain by Clays Ltd, Elcograf S.p.A

Papers used by Piatkus are from well-managed forests
and other responsible sources.

MIX
Paper from
responsible sources
FSC

To the mum with the never-ending to-do list –
this book is for you.

Contents

It is a truth, universally acknowledged, that the busiest mum in the playground is the one who is #thriving and #livingherbestlife.
Or is she?

Introduction

Does time (or a lack of it) make you panic? Do you always feel as though you are on the back foot, seemingly the only person on the planet who is always running late? Do you look around on a manic Monday morning and see other people suited, booted, calm and in control, sipping on their oat-milk lattes?

Perhaps you feel blinded by the overwhelm of having so much to do, but so little time. One thing is certain, though: you can't do everything on your list. You need to choose, and you need to choose wisely, or you'll get struck with the regret of precious time wasted.

You are not alone in feeling that time races by too fast for you to keep up. A lot of us will identify with the feeling of getting to the end of a day, possibly still in our pyjamas come dinner time, without really knowing what we have done with our time. All we know is that we feel as though we've been hit by a freight train and are exhausted.

Does that resonate with you? And do you also feel over-whelmed about how to best utilise any free time you have available? Imagine two whole hours of free time are stretch-ing out in front of you. You are faced with a decision: do you have a rest? Do the housework? Catch up with Netflix (#selfcare)? Phone your mum back?

Before you know it, it's forty-five minutes later and you haven't done a single thing.

Even if you are clear about the way you want to spend your precious free time, the mental load that comes with the territory of being a modern woman often means that your priorities are clouded by a never-ending to-do list. A woman's work is never done and all that!

Maybe you have been trying to go for a run all week but, no matter how hard you try, things keep cropping up, meaning you keep pushing your run to the bottom of your priority list, and going for that 5k never happens.

Maybe your boss asked you to stay later at work.

Maybe you had to take your kid to a minor injuries unit because they got a pea stuck up their nose.

Or maybe you finally carved out the time to go running, only to find you hadn't remembered to wash your kit.

If your to-do list is causing your brain to feel foggy, this book is for you. If you feel ground down by the weight of all your responsibilities – taking care of your family, running a household, succeeding in your career – this book is for you. If you wake up in the morning knowing that you have a lot to do, but the overwhelm of the lists ping-ponging around your head means that you can't see the wood for the trees, this book is for you. If it feels easier to just stick your head under the pillow, wishing you could press the pause button on being an adult, this book is *definitely* for you.

I recently took a straw poll over on my social media channels and a huge number of the people (mostly women) who responded all said that time was one of the things they felt they didn't have a grip on – and it's stressing them out. So, take heart: you are not alone in wishing that there were twenty-five hours in every day.

But time doesn't grow on trees; nor can we pause it like the girl from *Out of this World*. Old Father Time is very static. He has very definite boundaries that can't be stretched or extended. We have what we have. Time is finite and, with every second that passes, the time we have decreases.

I am not saying this to make you panic. I just want to show you the hard facts. I find a bit of tough love at the start of a self-help book is good for the soul.

While we can't pause time or pull an extra hour out of our backsides, what we can do is put some strategies in place to get this jungle of to-do lists and demands on our time under control. That's why I am here, and that is what we are going to start doing right now.

My hope is that, by the end of this book, you will have a new set of skills that will open up a whole new world of possibilities, ranging from getting the school run done on schedule (*with* your lippy on), all the way to finding the time to set up that longed-for business – or maybe, just maybe, carving out the time to write a book (that's me right now!).

So, why don't you grab a cup of tea and a couple of your favourite biscuits, settle in and let me tell you how I came to write a book all about time.

WHO AM I?

For those of you who are new here, this is my second book. My first, *The Organised Mum Method*, was written to help people gain control of the housework. It was written as a result of my own struggle to get it all done when I became a new mum. Those of you who have read it will know that I am not a naturally organised person. In fact, the idea of 'the organised mum' started out very tongue-in-cheek, as it was something that I was striving towards. In short, I was faking it to make it.

Growing up, I was never 'that girl': the one who had it all together, effortlessly gliding through life. I didn't have neatly covered textbooks with the sticky-back plastic stuck on so precisely that there wasn't a bubble in sight. (To this day, that skill continues to elude me.) I couldn't even get through the school day without putting a hole in my tights and I always felt like I was a work in progress.

I had to teach myself how to lead an organised life. It all started when I had my first child. Struck with postnatal anxiety, I thought that, in order for me to be a good mum, I had to have an immaculate home. I would clean for hours a day, literally wasting the early days of motherhood scrubbing the sinks and vacuuming the floors. Luckily, I recognised that I needed to change, and I created a cleaning method that meant I would get the cleaning done in just thirty minutes a day, five days a week (the weekends were purposefully kept housework-free). Without wanting to sound dramatic, I got my life back.

Everything I learned about keeping the household running (without the household running me) went into that first best-selling book, but that was only the first part of my story.

When my first marriage ended, I experienced being a single mum, and I know the time struggles that can go hand in hand with being the only responsible adult in the household. It is a pressure like no other. Not only do you start to have little to no time to yourself, but the irony is that now, more than ever, that 'me time' really matters. You need to look after yourself as there is no one else around to help you pick up the slack.

When I was a single mum, it was just me, Tom and Jonny, who were four years old and eighteen months old at the time. I was suddenly faced with challenges that I had never thought I would have to overcome, but it was through these challenges that I became a stronger and happier person.

At first, I struggled. I didn't eat (the 'divorce diet' helped me lose the last of the baby weight). I remember feeding Jonny in his highchair and crying; I remember phoning the solicitor and crying because I couldn't get the word 'divorce' out, hanging up with embarrassment. I remember feeling very cold all the time. It was the summer, so I guess I was in a state of shock.

But I was still a mum, and this meant that I couldn't totally sink, because I still had to function. I couldn't go to bed with a bottle of wine. I had to take Tom to the park and get him ready to start primary school. I had to change Jonny's nappy and make sure they were both happy, well fed and loved. As well as meeting the needs of my kids, I had to sort out other stuff, too. Suddenly, I had to work out how to cope financially on my own. I had to sell a house, find a new house to rent, run a business and find a new job that I could do from home (that's when I started writing – and I've never looked back!).

I decided I needed a plan of action. So, I came up with a way to cope. A way of being able to keep moving forward rather than sinking. I had already been using The Organised Mum Method (TOMM) before my marriage broke down to help me manage the housework, but I knew I needed something else. That's where The Organised Time Technique (TOTT) came in.

The Organised Mum Method was never just about having a clean house. It has become a way of life that has helped me to become the person that I wanted to be. Over the years, I have learned how to better balance my time, and The Organised Mum Method has become a small piece of a much larger technique: a technique that keeps my life turning without the wheels coming off.

And the rest of that technique is what I am going to be sharing with you in this book. I am going to give you the complete package that will help you go from feeling flustered to feeling fabulous.

I AM WRITING THIS BOOK BECAUSE YOU ASKED ME TO

This book is the result of helping tens of thousands of women over a number of years, not just as an antenatal teacher and a doula but also, in later years, through running the TeamTOMM Facebook group that has (at the time of writing) one hundred thousand members.

I wrote it because one of the most common questions I get asked is: 'How do I find the time to fit in The Organised Mum Method?'

At first it was just the odd question here and there, but pretty soon they were coming in thick and fast. It became clear that the biggest obstacle people were facing was not having enough time – not just to fit in the housework, but also to fit in everything else that needs doing in life.

This book is for all those stressed, overworked parents who are trying their best to balance all the things that come with the territory of raising a family – as well as trying to carve out a little bit of time for themselves.

How familiar is the image of the stressed-out, struggling mum caught up in the rat race? 'Wine o'clock' has become synonymous with the time of day when a mum can *finally* unwind, her life so hectic that her only hope is to turn to the gin (mother's ruin). A glass of something is seen as her only getaway car from the monotonous hamster wheel that is her day-to-day life: a tiny moment of freedom at the end of the long day.

Of course, there are lots of other things that we turn to as getaway cars to help us block out the monotony of the daily grind. It could be a glass of wine, but it could also be binge-watching Netflix shows or comfort eating a whole tube of Pringles at lightning speed. All these little escapes and coping mechanisms distract us from the problems that need fixing: a job we hate, a marriage in trouble, or just the sheer boredom that comes with running a home.

The struggling mum is the modern-day damsel in distress, but who is there to rescue her?

No one, that's who. We can't keep shoving more and more tasks into our days without expecting something to give. We have to rescue ourselves.

So, let's stop distracting ourselves with the usual coping mechanisms and getaway cars. Let's roll up our sleeves and fix the problems.

In the pages that follow I am going to introduce you to The Organised Time Technique, my master plan that will give you the tools – and the headspace – you need to create a framework for your life that means you will always know where you are supposed to be, what you are supposed to be doing, and when you are supposed to be doing it. And, more importantly, you will be able to find the time to do the stuff that makes you feel like yourself again.

How I wish that I'd had access to not only my first book when I was younger, but to this one, too. It would have helped me to streamline my life much earlier, meaning that I would have made far fewer mistakes. I hope that, by writing this book, I can help others to achieve more balance in their lives.

I hope you love it; I have written this book, with love, for all of you women out there who feel as though you are spinning far too many plates at once. After you have read it, please pass it on to a friend or family member and let's spread the love.

Are you ready? Let's gain control of the madness and get our lives running like clockwork.

1

Why are You Feeling So Overwhelmed?

Before I introduce you to The Organised Time Technique, there are a few bits of 'housekeeping' we need to take care of. In order for TOTT to work, you need to think about what's brought you to this book in the first place, so that you are as realistic as possible about why you are feeling so overwhelmed.

THE PRESSURE TO 'HAVE IT ALL'

As a young girl in the 1980s, my head was full of ambition. I was told that we were in a new, female-centric era and that we could have it all. I could have two point four children, a power-suit-worthy career and, if I had a microwave, I could be a great cook, too. All I had to do was remove the outer packaging, pierce the film lid several times, and a few minutes later my family would be bowled over by my culinary prowess.

As a teenager, I went to an all-girls' school. I learned how to sew a cushion, had a few cooking lessons in my food tech class (I learned how to make a Cornish pasty and meringues) and I was taught how to wire a plug. All good? Had I been given enough life skills to help me achieve 'she can have it all' nirvana? Sadly not.

It has been a few decades since my friends and I were told that we could be anything we wanted to be, go anywhere we wanted to go *and* raise a family, all while maintaining a successful relationship and impressive career.

But no one told us *how* we could have it all. And we didn't really ever question it: as naive and inexperienced teenagers, we just assumed it was possible because that's what we were told. Nobody ever sat us down and really analysed whether we *could* actually achieve everything. Nobody thought about how *thinking* we could have it all, but not quite being able to get there, might affect our mental health.

I am going to level with you. I believe that the idea that the modern woman can 'have it all' is an enticing mirage that has seduced most of us at one time or another. In my experience, heading out on an expedition to achieve everything and have the perfect life could see you losing yourself along the way. Because the perfect life simply does not exist: it's an unreachable goal.

Every day I see women who, upon seeing that they don't have the dream job, the dream house, the dream man, the impeccably behaved kids, the perfect gym body and the time to cook organic meals from scratch, feel as though they are failing. You might be one of them – I know I certainly was.

I am here to tell you that you are not failing. If you strive for this level of 'perfection' you will be trying to do too much. This is an impossible ideal that you are never going to make a reality.

I want to be very clear about what I mean by this. As women, we can be anything we want to be, we can go anywhere we want to go, but we cannot be *everything* to *everyone*; we cannot be 'perfect' in every area of our lives. If we try to be, all that happens is we burn ourselves out.

To truly break free, we need to completely rewrite the script. We need to add time-management to our list of skills, learn to accept that we can't do everything and prioritise the things that are most valuable to us.

THE DOMESTIC LOAD IS NOT EQUALLY SPLIT

Ninety-eight per cent of my followers on the social media channels I run are female. The figures don't lie. I'm not forcing women to follow me, and I'm not stopping men from pressing that follow button either. Believe me, I wish it was an equal split. But nearly one hundred per cent of the people who follow me are women, and they are all trying to find a way to do the housework, run a home, be a mum, do their day jobs and fit everything else into their lives. It speaks volumes.

All of these women are searching for a solution, desperately attempting to balance all of their competing responsibilities. Why does it fall to women to carry so much of the weight alone?

I know that this is a really tricky topic to navigate, but navigate it we must, and we must do it now. If not for us, then definitely for our daughters and sons. Because if we don't address it and talk about it now, it is inevitable that they will go on to face the same problems.

Daily I see many people (usually, but not always, women) on the TeamTOMM Facebook group who are trying to redress the balance in their homes. They feel as though they are doing more than their fair share of the domestic duties. Very often they feel put upon and can't see a way out of it. Resentment is building and they are stuck in a cycle where they find it easier to just do everything themselves rather than ask the people who they live with to pitch in – anything for a quiet life, hey?

Before I started to talk about The Organised Mum Method online, I was an antenatal teacher, a fourth-trimester teacher and a doula. I saw a lot of mums. At my busiest times, over one hundred mums a week would walk into my studio, some with newborns, others just about to have their first, second or maybe even third baby.

When I started my blog and my social media channels to talk about TOMM, I continued to speak to women, but this time my net widened and I was able to reach thousands of women, all over the world.

This puts me in a unique position. I have spoken to many, many mums over the years. I have made them coffee and cake and listened to their problems and frustrations in person, and now I lend a listening ear and a shoulder to cry on for many others over private messages online. This means I have got to know mums very well and I know what makes them tick.

And do you know the one thing that comes up all the time?

'Now that I have become a mum, I feel as though I am the domestic director in the home.'

Mums are usually the go-to person for:

- the groceries
- cooking dinner
- doing the laundry
- cleaning the house
- walking the dog
- and all other sorts of domestic drudgery that aren't listed in either the romantic vision of motherhood or the 'have it all' dream that we are sold

All of this can breed resentment. I mean, is there any wonder? So how does this unequal split happen?

As I have grown into a woman, had kids, got married, got divorced, got remarried, run businesses, worked in regular nine-to-five jobs and moved into writing, it has become very clear to me that, as modern women, we are facing some very hard choices. And these choices have consequences.

If we want to have kids, we are usually the ones that have to take a break from our careers and go on maternity leave. And, once again, the 'having it all' master plan unravels. Because it isn't quite as simple as we were once led to believe.

When someone (usually the woman) takes parental leave, keeping the household running slowly but surely starts to become lumped in with taking care of the child. In fact, it can become so intrinsically linked that it starts to become impossible to unpick the two. Very often, it happens without anyone (including the woman) even noticing.

You're sitting in the nursing chair feeding your newborn baby, thinking about the never-ending to-do list. The washing, the cleaning, the empty fridge that needs restocking. Your mind starts to wander, thinking of more and more stuff that needs doing. Sometimes it is quite literally staring you in the face as you eye up the pile of unfolded, clean washing on the kitchen table. So, to make yourself feel better and improve the environment around you, you just do it: you fold the laundry, you do the washing-up, you restock the fridge. Soon, it just becomes your new normal. All the while, you are losing sight of the fact that you were not taking parental leave to become a housekeeper; you were taking a break from your career to raise a child and to recover from childbirth.

And then comes the time when you decide if and when you want to return to work, another choice that has big consequences. Or maybe you don't have the luxury of a choice;

maybe your finances are such that the choice has been made for you and you have to go back to your old job, and soon.

This is where you reach another crossroads and you have to make the decision: to maintain the status quo and carry on with the domestic stuff (or try to); to get a cleaner (if you can afford one); or to have the conversation with your partner about making the domestic workload equal (assuming that your partner is willing to play ball).

And that conversation can be a hard one to have, because over the last few months, you have slipped into the role of taking care of the 'domestic stuff', and now you are asking your partner to share this workload with you. This means that they are now being asked to take on additional work – by you. This can make you feel guilty, and cause immediate feelings of panic that you are, in some way, not good enough; that you are failing as a mum and as a woman because you are having to ask for help. Weren't we told, way back when, that we could have it all?

And, oh yes, it also brings with it the threat of the dreaded caricature, the one we would all hate to become: the Nagging Wife.

It is an almost impossible situation and it is setting us up to fail. We are spinning all of the plates, inevitably dropping a few, and it is making us stressed and miserable. The Organised Time Technique is going to help you to rethink your situation, lighten the load you've unconsciously absorbed and carve out time for things that are most important to you.

HOW WE SPEND OUR DAYS

Go on, ask me what I did all day ... I dare you!
Working on social media, as I do, you come across some
amazing stories. This is one such tale. It is so poignant that I
have to share it with you.

One day on my Instagram stories, I was talking about the
fact that domestic work is one of those things in life that
nobody really pays any attention to – unless, of course, it isn't
getting done. Then everyone gets pretty vocal about it.

'Mum, where's my PE kit?'

'Mum, there's nothing in the fridge and I'm hungry!'

'Mum, there's no toilet roll!'

I received lots of replies and comments, with people nodding along in virtual agreement, agreeing that most domestic
duties are thankless tasks, but that they are entirely necessary
to keep a home running smoothly.

But one reply really struck a chord with me (and I have been
talking about it ever since). It was from a lovely TOMMer
(let's call her Maggie), and this is what she said:

> 'One day, I felt so underappreciated and fed up with
> everyone assuming that running a home was easy,
> that every time I did a job that was related to run-
> ning the house, I took a Post-it note and stuck it on
> the associated item. At the end of the day the house
> was full of Post-its!

There was one stuck on the TV saying: "I dusted this".
There was one next to the slow cooker, which had that night's dinner in it, saying: "I cooked this".
There was one on the fridge that said: "I filled this with food".
And so on and so forth . . . You get the picture.'

While the message from Maggie was light-hearted in tone, it does point to an underlying problem that many women face on a daily basis: not only is domestic work unpaid but, in some cases, its importance is hugely under-valued. As a result, it can be difficult to take a step back and work out what you've been doing all day. This problem is by no means a new one, and I'm sure we've all read countless blog posts and reports that have worked out how much a stay-at-home mum's salary would be if it was a paid role. We have also seen countless articles asking women not to try to judge whether they are working harder than other women, and we've all read pieces about stay-at-home mums versus working mums.

Look at it this way. You might not have:

- attended a board meeting
- brought about world peace
- made a million

But you *did*:

• wipe a snotty nose
• soothe a temperature
• referee a sibling squabble

... all while scrambling to finish putting together the Nativity costumes (and making dinner)!

That's a solid day's work in my eyes. It's really important that we *all* realise just how vital our contribution to the household and society is, and just how much we really are doing.

OK, cleaning the loos at home might not sound that impressive, but it helps you maintain the hygiene standards in your home. This helps to keep everyone healthy, which in turn enables you and the other adults in your home to go to work, and the kids to go to school. Keeping homes running smoothly is a very important cog in the big machine called society. The job might be different, but it does not mean that it is any less important.

Back in my doula days, I would often see new mums who were still in their dressing gown come midday. They would always apologise, probably worried that I would think that they had just been lounging about all morning watching breakfast TV without bothering to get dressed. But if these women had adopted the same strategy as Maggie and made a list of everything they had done that morning, I bet you that, as sure as eggs is eggs, that list would be as long as their arms.

It would have probably been full of things like:

- changed a nappy
- fed the baby
- unloaded the dishwasher
- changed a nappy
- reloaded the dishwasher
- fed the baby
- sterilised the bottles
- changed a nappy

I think you get the picture.

I (like many women) have experienced life as a stay-at-home mum, a work-from-home mum and a mum who works outside the home. All are equally challenging in their own unique ways.

When you are running the home and you are a stay-at-home parent, your place of work is your house: you can never escape it. You cannot shut the door on your work at 5 p.m. and not have to think about it again until the next day. Your work is all around you and, as a result, you can never switch off.

If you are a working mum, whether you work in the home or in an office, you finish your day job and then it's time to start *another* type of work.

So, I say: domestic CEOs, unite! We are all in this together. It's time to take back some time for ourselves. Consider this book a training course that will help you to become a kick-arse CEO of your home – the kind of CEO who spends Friday afternoons on the golf course!

2

It's Time to Make a Change

This is the part where we start to change our perspective and redress the balance. This is where we put systems in place so that we begin to feel less like the family scullery maid and more like the women we dreamed of becoming when we were young girls. You need to do this to make sure that your life doesn't slip by in one long to-do list. You need to try your very best to get off the hamster wheel and start actually living. By that, I mean you need to start living the life that you envisioned when you were younger – or a version of it, at least. (When I was younger, I dreamed that I was going to marry Mark Owen from Take That. Sadly, I have yet to find any systems that have allowed me to make this dream a reality, but there's still time – I'm ever the optimist.)

The first step in this process is recognising that the way

you are currently living your life isn't working. You need to give yourself permission to go against the grain and change things.

This is the first and most important step.

In the last chapter, we looked at some of the 'big picture' reasons for why we feel as though things aren't working and that we are juggling too many balls. Now we are going to take a really close look at what you do, every day, that contributes to making you feel completely overwhelmed. Understanding this will help you work out how to change the way you run your day-to-day life.

At times like this, I find it is best to always start with some hard facts and work from there. These facts are the very foundation of The Organised Time Technique.

- **Fact 1:** There are only twenty-four hours in a day: that's 1,440 minutes. We can't change that very stark, very hard fact.
- **Fact 2:** Our time has a hard boundary. If we run out of time, we can't get more.
- **Fact 3:** The only thing we can do is to learn how to use our time in the most efficient way possible. Otherwise, we just keep borrowing time from other parts of our lives to try to fit everything in. This can mean that we are forced to borrow from Peter to pay Paul, and this could see us taking time away from the things that are vital to our health and wellbeing, such as sleeping.

Anyone who has ever been sleep-deprived (and I guess this applies to almost everyone reading this book) will know that, when we lose sleep, we start to resemble a 'mombie' more and more every day. It makes things seem bleak and it becomes harder to function. This is one of the reasons you must safeguard the time you need to make sure you stay healthy, so that your body can function at its best.

Before we go any further, I want to make it clear that I am not going to show you how to shoehorn as much productivity into a twenty-four-hour period as you can. I am going to encourage you to make a decisive shift in attitude that not only gives you the time and space to do what you *have* to do, but also gives you the time to do what you *want* to do.

I just want you to let that message sink in.

A SHIFT IN ATTITUDE NOT ONLY GIVES YOU THE TIME TO DO WHAT YOU *HAVE* TO DO, BUT ALSO GIVES YOU THE TIME TO DO WHAT YOU *WANT* TO DO.

Read that sentence back to yourself.

Does that feel a bit indulgent? Does it seem a little bit naughty that we are considering planning in a decent chunk of self-care and self-development time, when it has been drummed into us that we are lucky to grab five minutes of peace when we go to the loo? If your answer to that is 'yes', this means that you *absolutely* have to start fighting back. Feeling guilty about the idea of taking time out for yourself is a sure sign that you are not doing it enough. You have to start working on strategies to find this time.

And that's why I'm here, to help you to do that with The Organised Time Technique.

I am going to go out on a limb and say I am pretty certain that, given the choice, none of us would choose to be complaining, coercing, bribing and – dare I say it – nagging our families to pitch in with the household duties, so that we can cut ourselves a bit of slack and take the time to have a bath and read a book. This is not the vision we had of our adult selves. If you had the choice, I'm pretty confident you would choose not to be strung out, stressed out and working at one hundred miles an hour, just to keep your head above water.

But in order to get to the point where you *can* have a bath in peace, you need to evaluate and clear your mind (and life) of the things that are getting in the way of you relaxing among the bubbles. In short, you need to get rid of the things that are no longer serving their purpose.

To do this, you need to thoroughly assess what is going on in your life and how you are spending your time. You need to do a Time Bootcamp. And when you look at the results of the Bootcamp, you need to be strong in your decisions, making sure that you are fair to yourself and that you don't allow yourself to be drawn into overworking because you think it is the 'right thing to do'.

OK, I'M ON BOARD, SO WHAT'S NEXT? THE ORGANISED TIME TECHNIQUE EXPLAINED

Before we dive head first into Bootcamp, I want to explain to you what The Organised Time Technique is all about.

The Organised Time Technique started as a small idea I had when I began to section off my time with The Organised Mum Method.

Before I became a mum, time really didn't mean anything more to me than making sure that I got to work on time and that I had my bum on the sofa for when *Friends* was about to start. In fact, I'm pretty certain that most us (if not all of us) can look back to before we became parents and marvel at how much spare time we actually had, blissfully unaware of how strapped for time we were going to be once we had some little humans to look after.

Oh, how the luxury of time is wasted on the carefree!

When I became a mum, I was struck with an overwhelming instinct to create the nicest home environment that I could for my new little family. I had given up my business (I owned a very successful fish-and-chip shop – I make the best mushy peas!) and, driven by my instincts, my focus firmly switched to my new role as a mum. And the inevitable happened. Just as we have already discussed, all of the domestic work started to land at my feet. At first, I happily accepted it. I am not sure if it was the novelty factor of trying to create the perfect home, or the fact that I was enjoying a new challenge, or a combination of the two, but I launched myself into my new role of stay-at-home mum with relish. I even bought myself a cleaning kit that included a matching pink apron, pink rubber gloves and a pink scrubbing brush (how I cringe about that now!).

I am a bit of an all-or-nothing sort of person. I go from zero to one hundred per cent pretty damn quickly (it can be both a blessing and a curse). Pretty soon, my eagerness to be the best mum and wife that I could be turned into an obsession, one which was taking over many hours of my day. I decided to compartmentalise the cleaning into thirty-minute chunks, and TOMM was born. I created an eight-week rolling method of thirty minutes a day that meant that my whole house got the full treatment over each two-month cycle. It was efficient, it kept me focused, and it compartmentalised the cleaning so that I didn't need to think about it any more than I had to. It meant that I was able to get my obsessive cleaning under control and start to actually enjoy all of the other things that come with the territory of being a mum.

Very soon, I realised how powerful the technique of sectioning off time was, and I started to use it in other areas of my life as well. I would set the timer to get the paperwork done, or to complete some life admin that I had been putting off for ages.

I clearly remember one particularly challenging time of my life (just after my first marriage had broken down), where the technique proved to be worth its weight in gold. The breakdown of my marriage had floored me, and I was left devastated, feeling like my life had been turned inside out. I needed to look after two very small children, keep a business going, run a home, reorganise my finances and go through a mentally draining divorce. I was utterly overwhelmed.

I knew that I needed to pull myself up by my bootstraps, and I started by putting some practical strategies in place. I used to set my timer every day for thirty minutes and make myself do something practical that was going to help me get my life back on track. I used the time to help me power through the jobs that I wasn't relishing the thought of doing; things like changing the bills back into my name and working through my finances. It was so powerful because these smaller chunks of time didn't overwhelm me. It meant that I was able to get a lot done without it impacting on my already fragile state of mind.

I started to sort out my life, thirty minutes at a time.

It was so successful that I stuck with the technique and TOMM organically expanded to become just one piece of The Organised Time Technique. This is what I still use, to this day, to help me manage my time and structure my life.

And just like TOMM has stuck with me throughout the years, proving to be invaluable through thick and thin, TOTT has been the same. Over the years, TOTT has allowed me to start businesses, earn a decent income while working from home, work on twenty-four-hour call as a doula, raise three children and write (first one and now two) books. Without TOTT by my side, I know that achieving all of this would have been so much harder, if not impossible.

It allowed me to put systems in place that helped me to juggle the time struggles that come hand in hand with being a woman who works full-time, is a mother to three kids, a wife to a lovely man and the owner of a *very* cute and lively Jack Russell, who needs regular walks.

TOTT is still with me now, helping me to navigate from day to day and cope with the twists and turns that life likes to throw at us. My life isn't perfect: no one's is. My husband and I still come across hurdles but I always know that TOTT has my back and, if things go a little off-piste, I can always count on it to help get me back on track.

I know that lots of people in my online TOMM community (TOMMers!) have recognised the power of sectioning off their time, especially for tasks that you are not too keen on doing. People contact me regularly letting me know that the TOMM technique of setting a time limit and sticking to it not only motivates them to get stuff done, but also helps them to break down overwhelming tasks into smaller, bite-sized pieces. Clearing out the loft doesn't seem so much of a daunting job when you view it as a series of thirty-minute chunks that you can come back to another time.

OK, let's get down to business and break down what The Organised Time Technique is all about and, more importantly, what it can do for *you*.

The Organised Time Technique, broken down

I want you to start to look at your day as a series of time units. Not hours and minutes, but units. I want you to do this so that you start to see your time as something that is finite, something that can – and will – run out.

It is totally up to you how you break down your twenty-four hours. You might want to split it into twenty-four one-hour units, forty-eight thirty-minute units or go even further and manage your life in ninety-six fifteen-minute units. Personally, I have always found the thirty-minute unit to be the most adaptable and easy to use, so that's the unit we are going to use in this book. This means that you will have forty-eight units to play with in one twenty-four-hour period.

That is your starting point.

These are all the units you have; you can't borrow more or store them up to use tomorrow or next week. Your units do not roll over: they go up in a puff of smoke when the clock strikes midnight. What you get is what you get; that is all there is. Use them or lose them. It sounds harsh, but it's true.

Time is money

I want you to think of your time just as you would your hard-earned cash. You need to start spending your time just as wisely. You wouldn't squander your monthly pay cheque; I want you to be just as protective over your time (if not more so). And, if you use your time wisely, a fantastic knock-on effect of TOTT is that you can actually start to grow your income and increase your pay cheque (we'll see an example of this in chapter four).

Before we dive into the mechanics of TOTT, we need to start working out how you are going to use your time.

To do this, we need to go right back to basics. Enter the Time Bootcamp!

TIME BOOTCAMP

If you already follow TOMM, this next step is going to be very familiar to you. You are going to embark on a Time Bootcamp. This is the first step of The Organised Time Technique process and it will enable you to work out where your time-management weaknesses and strengths currently lie. The areas in your life where you are not making the best use of your time should soon start to become obvious.

The Bootcamp will reveal whether your time struggles are down to mismanagement, lack of motivation or simply that you are trying to fit too much in – or a combination of all three.

Visualise your day as a bucket. You start each day with a full bucket of time to spend on all the tasks you need to do. All of those tasks take time. If your bucket isn't sturdy and has a few holes, then it will start to leak, and you will lose time. It is your job now to find the holes and fix any leaks in the bucket. You can't just keep working with the same leaky bucket or you will find yourself back at square one; leaking time and energy.

No one likes a leaky bucket!

Now, I know that, for many of you, this is going to be a very frustrating part of the process. No doubt you are raring to get cracking and map out your days. Believe me, I know that the temptation will be to get going as quickly as you can, but please trust me when I say completing the Time Bootcamp is *vital*. In order for TOTT to work properly, you can't miss this section out. It is the cornerstone of the whole process, forming the foundations of the rest of the technique.

For those of you who *still* want to skip this part (I can see you!), please heed my warning. If you do a half-hearted job on Bootcamp, you will end up with an ineffective TOTT plan and you will have to start all over again. You will actually have wasted your time, which is the opposite of what we are trying to achieve.

How to Bootcamp your time

Over the next week, you are going to write down EVERYTHING (and I mean EVERYTHING) that you spend your time on. From how long it takes you to travel into work in the morning, all the way down to how long you spend scrolling through your social media feed. It all has to be recorded.

How you track your time is going to be up to you, but the most important thing is that you are honest with yourself. There is a very good reason you are reading this book and that is probably because you want to be more efficient in the day-to-day running of your life. The only way you are going to find out where the problems lie is by being really honest with yourself about how your time is currently being spent and why your days are not going as smoothly as you would like them to.

A word to the wise: once you start to notice the areas that are causing your bucket to leak, you might feel uncomfortable or, dare I say it, a little bit embarrassed. Please don't let this stop you. Please be as honest with yourself as you possibly can. Sometimes it takes a slight shift in perspective, or for someone else to reflect a problem back to you (that'll be me!) before you can see it for yourself. This isn't your fault; you haven't done anything wrong. Be kind to yourself and know that, by reading this book and starting this process, you are doing the very best you can. Trust me, you've got this.

OK, let's begin! Over the next seven days, I would like you to document the way you spend your time.

For example:

- How long it takes you to get ready in the morning.
- How long the school run takes.
- How much sleep you are *really* getting.
- How much time you are spending on social media – yes, we are going there! You need to make a note of how much time that TikTok scroll-hole costs you!

Remember, you need to commit to being brutally honest in this process. If you're not honest, the only person you are going to be cheating is yourself.

Hints and tips for Bootcamp

Trust the process

To the busiest among you, it might seem counterproductive to be adding yet another task into an already chock-a-block week. For some of you, jotting down how long you are spending running from one meeting to another will seem like a step too far. It might even feel as though you are *wasting* time. Please trust me when I say that, if you fall into this group, you are one of the people who need TOTT the most. Look at spending that extra time in the Bootcamp phase as an investment that will pay dividends when you put your TOTT plan together.

Be accurate

It is really important that you are accurate when you note down how long things are taking you. A little later on, when you start to create your TOTT plan, you will be relying on these results to properly work out how many units to assign to tasks. You won't be able to assign the right number of units if you haven't noted things down properly. Be your future friend and make sure you record things accurately. Now is not the time for a guesstimate. It is crucial that you actually go through the process properly, rather than just sitting down and guessing how long things take. If you guess, you are at risk of either overestimating or underestimating the time different things take.

Don't finish early

The chances are that, fairly quickly, you will start to see obvious places where you are wasting time, or places where you have severely over- or underestimated the amount of time that you spend on certain things. When you start to notice these, the temptation can be to pack up and finish Bootcamp early, because you think you have unveiled the reasons for why you are struggling so much with time-keeping. But you *must* keep pressing on for the full week, because you will probably unearth yet more areas where you can improve.

Don't overthink it

I want you to live your life as normally as you can. If you find yourself spending twenty minutes sitting in your car on the driveway before you go back into the house after work, staring into space and enjoying the quiet, make sure you write it down. TOTT isn't a plan that will have you working like a machine to try and squeeze as much productivity out of your day as possible. It is about putting together a balanced approach to your days that will allow you the time you need to rest and do the things that make you happy. All of these little moments need to be noted down.

Don't judge yourself

As you go through the process, you will notice areas where you are wasting time, and you'll probably identify parts of your life where you are taking on far too much. Being hard on yourself and passing judgement on your decisions won't help. Be patient with yourself and feel encouraged by the fact that you are able to recognise areas where you can improve. Trust that TOTT is going to give you the tools you need to do that.

Keep your notes somewhere really accessible
This is going to sound really obvious but, in order to record as much of your time as you can, you are going to need to keep your time record with you everywhere you go. Using a notes app on your phone is perfect for this. If you have ever counted calories, you will no doubt see a correlation between calorie-counting and time-tracking. Both processes require every single thing to be noted – and they don't work if you cheat!

Choose a normal week
This one is fairly self-explanatory. There is zero point choosing to do your Bootcamp in the week between Christmas and New Year, as it won't give you an accurate representation of what your life is like.

Remember to reassess
It is worth remembering that the results of Bootcamp will be different for all of us. Indeed, the results of a Bootcamp you complete this week could be different to another one you might do in a few months. Your current life circumstances will have a huge impact on the outcome of your

Bootcamp, as well as what time of year it is: lots of factors come into play.

This is why I recommend doing regular Bootcamps. Reassessing your time a couple of times a year helps to keep things running as smoothly as possible, ensuring that you are still making the right decisions to keep your life running like clockwork. I find the best times for a good Time Bootcamp are January and August (although not when you are sitting on a sunlounger in the Costa Del Sol!).

Each and every one of us will face our own unique challenges. You might have newborn triplets; you might be caring for a relative; or you might have just become a single parent. There are many situations that can put additional strains on your time.

Here is my current time challenge: I am writing this book during the Covid-19 outbreak in the UK in 2020. Never in our lifetime have we experienced anything like this, and never before has my time budget been so stretched. Mike and I are both working full-time jobs from home; we are home-educating our three children aged four, eleven and thirteen (because all of the schools have closed to fight the spread); and the UK is in lockdown, meaning we all have to stay indoors as much as possible for what could be weeks (maybe months!). If TOTT can withstand this, I promise you, it can withstand anything you throw at it. And yes, I am writing this with a large glass of wine next to me. God knows I need it.

GEM'S TOP TIP!

If you need an emergency intervention and need your time crisis sorted *now* (maybe you don't have time to record your comings and goings for a week), this quick exercise can help.

Sit down and write a list of everything that you have going on at the moment. Write absolutely everything down, then systematically work your way through the list and start culling. Start with the things that can either wait, be delegated or dropped altogether. This will leave you with your list of priorities and show you where your focus should lie. This will help to bring back clarity to your frazzled brain.

Pay attention to details

Your Bootcamp notes don't have to be fancy or complicated. All you need to do is commit to carrying around a small notepad and pen or using a notes app on your phone. What matters is *what* you record, not *how* you record it. The best Bootcamp notes aren't the ones that are on the prettiest notepaper with fancy lettering and colours. Often, the best Bootcamp notes are the ones that are listed on a dog-eared notepad: not the prettiest to look at, but the most useful because they pay attention to the *detail*.

When it comes to Bootcamp, you will find that the devil is in the detail. As you are going about your daily tasks, the more information you can add to your notes, the better. Make sure you track your emotions as well, as this will help you to identify your hotspots. Knowing how your emotions and energy levels track in relation to your day will be crucial information for later on when you are planning out your days, TOTT style! If you feel stressed at certain points in your day, make sure that you record that, and why it is you think you feel that way.

Maybe you had not allowed yourself enough time to cook dinner in between school pick-up and dropping the kids off at karate, so that, by the time dinner was ready, they had to eat it in the car on the way to practice, leaving you feeling demoralised and like it was hardly worth the bother cooking from scratch in the first place! It would have been a hell of a lot easier to just bung a pizza in the oven. Your heart was in the right place, but the time available to you didn't allow for the execution. TOTT will help you to unravel all of this.

Noting everything down in as much detail as you can will mean that you will notice both the emotional and the practical roadblocks that are getting in your way.

You might find that your Bootcamp notes become more of a journal and you find out more about yourself than you first expected. That's OK: it is all part of your TOTT journey.

Here is an example of what your notes for a Monday morning might look like:

Monday morning – term time

7 a.m   *Woke up (didn't feel very refreshed – went to bed too late). Went downstairs for coffee, vitamins, let the dog out*

7.15 Woke the kids. Showered (miss not being able to shower in peace!)

7.30 Kids hungry, made them breakfast (had planned to make breakfast at 8am)

7.45 Back upstairs to finish getting ready. Felt rushed/ stressed as could hear kids squabbling downstairs (miss getting ready in peace!)

8am Eat breakfast while trying to cajole kids to get ready

8.15 15-min quick tidy before leaving the house at 8.30

Felt stressed – no head space!

BOOTCAMP IS OVER. NOW WHAT?

Well, for starters, can we please just take a moment to recognise that you have taken a massive step towards regaining control, not only of your days, but also your life. Give yourself a big pat on the back.

You have completed the first and most important step in the TOTT process. Your Time Bootcamp is done and you should now be able to see some very obvious areas in your life where you have been not been managing your time as efficiently as you could. Now is the time to assess your results and to work out what type of timekeeper you are.

WHAT TYPE OF TIMEKEEPER ARE YOU?

The overachiever

If you find that you are trying to fit far too much into your day and you climb into bed in the evening berating yourself for not getting through your ambitious to-do list, then you are an overachiever. You're probably guilty of trying to wring as much out of the hours as you possibly can, but all that happens is that you feel exhausted and wrung-out yourself.

Let's look at an overachiever's typical Monday morning (spoiler alert: they try to fit a lot in!).

TYPICAL OVERACHIEVER'S MORNING

We are with Carrie. Carrie is a single mum with three school-age kids. She runs her own business from home. She has lofty plans for her business and is willing to work her fingers to the bone to get there. She is also head of the PTA.

5 a.m. I have been getting up early as I read that some of the world's most successful people rise with the lark to get a head start on the day. I had planned on spending an hour on emails and some yoga before the kids woke up. But the eldest woke up early and made such a racket that the youngest two were

up shortly after, which means I didn't finish my emails – let alone do any yoga. Felt resentful and a failure before my day had started. Surely it shouldn't have to be this hard?

6 a.m. Gave in and started to flit around the house doing bits and bobs: laundry, checking on my business social media accounts. Got a text from my friend asking me if I had a spare PE shirt as her son had lost his. Assumed she needed it today, so went into loft and found it.

7 a.m. Felt guilty that I hadn't been paying attention to the kids while I was in the loft, so made them some blueberry pancakes; went down well but the mess took ages to clean up. Cleaned kitchen and got kids ready for school (still in yoga kit).

8 a.m. Had 15 minutes spare, so managed to fit in a quick yoga flow. Wasn't that great, though, as kids were noisy and I felt distracted. Felt like it was a waste of time and I probably would have been better off doing something more constructive instead.

8.30 a.m. Left for school (still in yoga kit), dropped off kids. Headed straight to the office to do some PTA admin. This should have taken 20 minutes max, but I got side-tracked because the office manager asked me to help carry some

▶

boxes into the hall for assembly. (Should not have worn yoga kit to school as it always gives the impression that I am a lady of leisure when really I need to get back home ASAP and pack orders for work.)

10 a.m. Finally made it home to start work but already running about an hour behind schedule. Felt stressed and annoyed with myself that I can't keep up.

The key characteristics of the typical overachiever are:

- You are the ultimate multi-tasker.
- You find it hard to say no.
- You would hate anyone to think of you as lazy.
- You are competitive by nature.
- You try to squeeze as much into your day as possible.
- You go through periods of feeling completely burned out or overwhelmed.
- You pride yourself on being busy.
- When you do have a moment to yourself, you don't know what to do with it.
- You rarely feel as though you get much headspace.
- Your brain feels full to the gunnels of to-do lists.
- Talking of lists . . . you love a good list!

How TOTT will help

Going through this process will be a real eye-opener for you. You will probably be shocked at how much you are trying to get done. If you have often wondered why it is that everyone else seems to have time for lie-ins at the weekend or seems to be able to sit down and read a book while you are running around like the proverbial blue-arsed fly, then it should have all become a lot clearer to you during the Bootcamp process.

I am not going to lie to you: you are going to have to make some hard decisions. You are going to have to start to drop tasks or delegate them. You are going to have to be ruthless and learn to defend your time with the ferocity of a rottweiler.

I am going to teach you how to value your own health and wellbeing just as highly as you value what other people think of you. Not only this, but you are going to have to challenge your own perception of what it means to be successful. TOTT will teach you that not all rewards come in the shape of promotions and quantifiable achievements. You are going to start to make time for the lie-ins, the baths and the book-reading sessions. To put it simply, TOTT will give you back your freedom.

The dreamer

Dreamers are a bit of a paradox. Just like overachievers, they love a good list. They love to plan and strategise. But they put so much energy and love into the planning phase that they rarely have time to actually *do* the things they've planned;

and, if they are honest with themselves, *doing* the things isn't half as much fun as *planning* the things.

Doing is boring; dreaming and planning are where their passion lies.

A typical dreamer is the sort of person who would spend most of their revision time at school devising the most beautiful colour-coordinated revision plan, mapped out to perfection, but never actually get around to doing any of the revision because they had exhausted themselves with the planning process!

Dreamers are the group who are the most likely to be a flight risk during the TOTT process. They will love planning how they are going to spend their time, but the part that they will find tricky is when they have to stick to that plan. It will prove to be a big challenge, but don't fret – I've got your back!

Let's take a trip to a typical dreamer's Monday morning to see what their Bootcamp notes might look like.

TYPICAL DREAMER'S MORNING

We are with Rachel. Rachel is a new mum. She is starting to feel like herself again after the birth of her son and she is excited about this new chapter in her life. She has built up the perfect image of motherhood in her head: she has read all the books and written down all the schedules, and dreams of her maternity leave being filled with her smiling at her baby as her visions of motherhood become a reality.

4.30 a.m. Wake up for the early morning feed. My antenatal group are all meeting up at the park and I can't wait to see them all. Text them while I am feeding and suggest a picnic as it is going to be a lovely day. I decide to bake some cakes. Excited for a summer picnic!!

5.30 a.m. Put little one down for nap, sit down and plan what I am going to bake. Get side-tracked trying to work out which cake would be the best and lose track of time. Before I know it, nap time is over and it's time for another feed!!

7.00 a.m. Still not dressed, two feeds down. Start texting friends to see what they are taking to the park. Plan little one's outfit.

8.30 a.m. Jump in the shower. Pop little one in bouncer and I get dressed. I still can't quite achieve the glowing new mum look yet and spend some time (15 minutes) scrolling through Instagram to get outfit inspo. Feel a bit rubbish that I can't fit in my jeans yet and pick my usual uniform of breast-feeding friendly tea dress, trainers and big pants. Look up a weight-loss plan, scroll through the rules and feel my mood

▶

drop instantly. I decide it is not for me. Remind myself that I am a new mum. Might try a baby bootcamp instead. I look up local classes.

9.30 a.m. Panic as I have not started baking yet. Set about rushing through the recipe while trying to settle little one at the same time. Feel frustrated that the other mums make it look like a blissful and easy job. I feel sweaty and harassed!! Wish I had the time to spend a lazy morning baking.

10.30 a.m. Text friends to say I am running late as I need to feed little one before I leave. While feeding I sit and try to plan dinner for tonight. Want to try and reconnect with husband, so want something fancy. Drive to the meet-up planning tonight's menu in my head.

11.30 a.m. Arrive at the park. Friends are all there. Feel really happy to see them but frustrated I haven't had the picture-perfect morning that I had imagined. Little one cried the whole way here and is still really unsettled. It starts raining so we decamp to the coffee shop. Cakes go uneaten (we aren't allowed to eat our own food in the coffee shop). Leave feeling deflated and exhausted. Might not bother making dinner later.

The key characteristics of a typical dreamer are:

- You have a fondness for stationery and bullet journals.
- You get excited about starting a new diary or project but never keep it up for more than a couple of weeks.
- You love strategy meetings at work (you never moan about having meetings about meetings).
- You prefer to look at the bigger picture rather than getting caught up with the smaller details.
- You very rarely finish projects.
- You get disheartened easily when things don't go to plan.

How TOTT will help

Sticking to TOTT is going to help you finally achieve the things that you have been dreaming about all this time. I do not doubt that you have grand plans and, by following TOTT, you will make significant steps towards achieving them.

Often your stumbling block has been putting your plans into practice. The sheer overwhelm of your lofty ambitions can put paid to your journey to success before you have even started. I am going to show you how to get to your goals, one time unit at a time, without getting overwhelmed.

The spendthrift

This is probably one of the easiest types of timekeeper to diagnose. The spendthrift has no idea where all their time goes. They get to the end of the day with no idea how they whiled away the hours and can't understand why they are still in their dressing gown at 7 p.m.

A typical spendthrift will be late for most things and be fairly relaxed about timekeeping in general. Watches are usually seen as decorative rather than a useful tool, and clocks might still be an hour out from the last time they were meant to have been put forward or back.

A spendthrift's morning Bootcamp notes might look like this.

TYPICAL SPENDTHRIFT'S MORNING

For this example, we are with Gill, who is playing out the typical morning scenario of many a working mum with kids. Gill is married with two kids at school (aged six and eight). Her husband works long days in the nearest city. He leaves home early to commute and gets back for dinner.

Gill is a typical spendthrift with her time in the mornings, guilty of pressing the snooze button on her alarm a little too often. When she does finally lift her head from the pillow, she is faced with a mountain to climb if she's going to get everyone out of the door on time and in one piece. This leaves her exhausted and feeling like she has already done a full day's graft before she even gets to work.

Set alarm for 6.30 a.m. but ended up getting up at 6.55 a.m. It felt really hard to open my eyes this morning, the bed was just too comfy for me to even contemplate getting up! I left it until the last possible minute, enjoying as much as I could of the duvet before I had to face the reality of being an adult. (I enjoy this time as it is the only chance I get to wrap my head around the day ahead.)

7–7.30 a.m. I showered and dressed and got the kids up at the same time. I didn't really have enough time to do my make-up (which is one of my goals – to get to work with lipstick and mascara on my face at the same time). This left me feeling resentful and it wasn't even 8 a.m.! Getting ready at the same time as the kids isn't working.

7.30–8.15 a.m. Got the kids dressed and downstairs for breakfast. Waved goodbye to Steve (felt resentful of him having a nice peaceful commute and not having to worry about getting Weetabix thrown at him over the table – then felt guilty for feeling resentful). Had a battle finding the kids' clean shirts, so this probably wasted a good few minutes. Went online to order some spares, saw there was a sale on and spent 10 minutes scrolling through the bargains.

▶

8.15 a.m. Left for school, leaving the house in a bit of a state, already dreading dealing with the dried-on Weetabix! Quick chat with a couple of the parents at school gates.

8.45 a.m. Drove to work, running late due to not allowing for traffic and losing track of time chatting in the playground. Hadn't had breakfast. Had planned to grab one of the cereal bars from the stash in my desk drawer but got called into a meeting as soon I got to the office. Embarrassing tummy rumbles until 10 a.m. when I could finally have something to eat.

We all know a spendthrift. They are the one whose friends know to tell them that an event is happening half an hour earlier than it actually is, just so that they'll actually turn up on time.

Spendthrifts and overachievers are polar opposites of each other.

Key characteristics of a spendthrift are:

- You tend to leave everything until the last minute.
- Projects are often left until the eleventh hour, meaning that they never turn out quite as well as you wanted them to.
- You have little patience and find it hard to concentrate on things for a decent length of time.

- You often arrive late.
- The snooze button on your alarm clock gets a lot of use.
- You usually severely underestimate the amount of time things will take.

How TOTT will help

Ahhh, the spendthrift. TOTT is going to change your life. Not only that – it will also change the lives of others around you. During this process you are going to figure out the barriers that are stopping you from achieving what you want to in life.

I am going to help you to identify the weak spots that cause you to lose focus, and I am going to give you a toolkit that means you will be able to effortlessly achieve more without feeling as though you have embarked on a whole new lifestyle.

3

Identifying Your Time-Suckers

Now that you have completed Bootcamp, you should have a good idea of where your time budget is being spent. And now we can start moving you forward.

The beauty of TOTT is that it is not rigid: it is flexible enough to be adapted to anyone's lifestyle. Even a Premier League footballer could follow TOTT if they wanted to; come to think of it, so could Beyoncé, for that matter!

I will give you the framework so that you can build your very own version of TOTT.

Before we dive straight into developing your TOTT plan, I want us to talk about some of the most common things that are leeching away your precious time (some of the things that are putting the holes in your bucket). In this section we are going to take a deeper look at some of the most common reasons that cause us to misuse or waste our precious time and how we can start to put measures in place to ensure that our time is balanced between self-care, work, family and all the other important parts of our lives.

We're not looking at specific tasks that take up time here (we'll come on to those in the next chapter). This is more about looking at any unhelpful thoughts, feelings and behaviours that might be throwing you off track.

THE TYPICAL TIME-SUCKERS

Your phone and social media

This is a biggie and I know that it will come as no surprise to you that you are probably spending far too much time on your phone. I know that, for many of us (me included), our phones provide an important link to our work, our friends and our hobbies. So much of the information that we digest comes to us via our phones. We often receive work emails on our phones or use them to take bookings from clients; many of us are part of work WhatsApp groups, too. I find that mobile phones are both a blessing and a curse. We live in an age where we are bombarded with information twenty-four seven, and our phones are some of the main sources. Our mobile phones and the associated social media apps that we store on them are, by far, among the worst time-suckers of our days. They are glued to us almost constantly; some of us even sleep with our phones next to us, especially when they also double up as our alarm clocks.

It is almost impossible to pick up your phone and not spend more time on it than you had initially intended to. How often have you picked up your phone to find out the time, only to put it down a few minutes later having checked a new message that pinged up, later realising that you never actually checked the time after all? This is so common – I know that I am guilty of it. I think it's fair to say that there is an element of anxiety surrounding phones (and technology in general, for that matter). We feel a need to know that we are up to date with the world's comings and goings so that we don't miss out (hello there, FOMO!). Each of the timekeeping personalities we discussed in the previous chapter will get caught in the phone trap: over-achievers answer emails well into the night; dreamers plan out their goals, download *all* the apps and gain inspo from their social media feeds; and spendthrifts will easily fall down a scroll-hole, finding themselves watching cat videos when they should be leaving for the school run. But what can we do to balance our need for information with making sure that the use of our phone doesn't have a negative impact on our time?

- Download an app on your phone to track the average number of hours you spend on it each day. The first time you see that number, it can be quite a shock – it certainly was for me. I do a lot of my work on social media so I knew it would be high, but it was still far higher than I expected. At the time of writing, I use the Screen Time app on my iPhone.

- If your work emails come through to your phone, compartmentalising your time between your job and your home life is going to prove tricky. You might have spent ten hours in the office already today but, if your phone pings just as you are about to sit down to dinner, it can be hard to settle down to eat until you know what the latest email says. That fear that you are missing something urgent always rears its head. Try muting your phone at a certain time each day by putting it on 'do not disturb' mode. Tell colleagues, family and friends that, if something is urgent, they need to phone you rather than email. I also recommend getting into the habit of scheduling any emails to be sent during work hours. That way, if you do ever need to catch up on some extra work in the evenings, you can do so without impacting on your colleagues' relaxation time. Maybe you can even ask your colleagues to do the same. This will heavily reduce the amount of out-of-office-hours phone pings, and is an absolute godsend for flexible workers.

- Only check your phone at designated intervals during the day. Sometimes, checking our phones can be so habitual that we don't even notice how often we do it. Weaning yourself out of the habit can be easier said than done. A great thing to try is to make a promise to yourself to only check your phone at certain times: this could be every fifteen minutes, every half-hour or every hour. The result is that, when you do check your phone, you will be doing so more mindfully and with intention.

• Organise your home screen into sections. This is something that I have done for a while and it works a treat. I have set up three home screens on my phone: one for work, one for life admin and one for lifestyle and health. The apps associated with these sections are filed away in folders on the relevant home screen. This means I am able to compartmentalise my phone into 'life zones' and it stops me from checking work apps at times when I am not working, like at the weekend. The work apps are filed away in the work folder rather than being on full view, and the fact that they aren't mixed in with the other apps on my phone means that I have to make the mindful choice to open the work folder – they're not just staring at me from the home screen.

• Turn off push notifications for everything but the essentials. This one more or less speaks for itself. Your phone will ping less and will therefore be much less likely to distract you.

Procrastination

Definition: *to delay or postpone action; to put off doing something.*

Are you prone to procrastination? I think we all are in some ways, but this is real spendthrift territory. And it is truly one of the peskiest hurdles to get over when we're trying to get stuff done. It's so easy to keep pushing that monotonous paper-shredding task or that awkward phone call to the bottom of your to-do list. But, deep down, we all know that it's better to just get it done: not only so that we can tick the task off our lists, but also because getting it done will free up valuable headspace, as we are no longer *thinking* about doing it (especially if it is a task that is causing us stress or anxiety). I always find that, once I've done the thing that I didn't want to do, it feels as though a massive weight has been lifted off my shoulders, bringing with it some much-needed mental clarity and freedom. A great way of keeping your procrastination gremlins at bay is to make it part of your daily routine to get the worst jobs done first thing in the morning. Getting the horrible stuff out of the way early doors means that, from a psychological point of view, the worst part of your day is already over and done with.

Self-sabotage and overthinking

I am a worrier; I worry when there is nothing to worry about! It is something that I know a lot of people struggle with. Do you worry too much about what others are doing or what others think about you? Little things, like becoming preoccupied with why a colleague seems to be getting more opportunities than you, or spending time scrolling through Instagram, longing for the body of a fitness influencer, are not only a big waste of time (and bad for your self-esteem), they also don't help you to progress towards your goals. All of us – but particularly overachievers – have to be careful not to get sucked into spending more time reading about, thinking about or talking about other people than we do thinking and working on ourselves and our own lives.

One of the most common ways in which we can get caught in this trap is through social media, gossip forums and gossip magazines. Social media can often turn from a healthy form of motivation to something a lot less positive. Say you are following a fitness influencer and you use their account to gain inspiration and tips while you embark on your own fitness journey, but you soon find yourself comparing yourself to them, spending so much of your valuable time watching them lead their life that you are not living your own life. If you feel as though you have more than a healthy level of interest in something, and that it is stopping you from actually getting out there and living, now is the time to take a step back. Social media can be addictive, and it can have a negative impact on your mental health. Please speak to someone and seek help if necessary.

In addition to the constant bombardment from our phones, throw in the pressure of being the perfect hostess at Christmas, planning the perfect kids' birthday party, always keeping one eye on what Karen from accountants is up to ... and we are faced with a world of needless, exhausting self-sabotage.

THERE ARE ONLY SO MANY HOURS IN A DAY

The refusal to come to terms with the fact that there are only so many hours (or units) in your day is a major obstacle that a lot of people struggle with. We live in a fast-paced world and we are constantly bombarded by thoughts, ideas and suggestions for how other people think we should be living our lives. One quick flick through a magazine or a brief glance at your phone can you leave you in a bit of a spin: incoming messages and suggestions about anything and everything, from making green smoothies and acai bowls to being a #mumboss and #slayingtheweek. This is where so many of us – again, overachievers in particular – come unstuck. We become a bit like rabbits in the headlights, blinded by the constant and overwhelming bombardment of what we 'should' be doing.

Stay in your lane

Let's take an example that lots of us will be familiar with: the school playground. Imagine that there are four mums, all having a quick chat just before school pick-up time. For illustrative purposes, let's give them all a name. We have Rachel, Monica, Phoebe and Janice (see what I've done there?). Indulge me on this and just bear with me: all will become clear soon.

Let's have a look at the four mums and their strengths.

Rachel

Rachel is really into her fashion. She always looks amazing, wearing all of the latest clothes and trends. You would never see her rocking up to school without a full face of make-up, hair done and looking anything less that perfectly polished – ever!

Monica

Monica is head of the PTA; her organisational skills know no bounds. She is the one that everyone messages in a panic at 8.00 a.m. to make sure that they have not missed the school email about non-uniform day. She is never late, and you can always depend on her to know what is going on.

Phoebe

Phoebe is a yoga teacher. She always has the most amazing, glowing skin, which she puts down to her devotion to green, leafy vegetables. She always looks relaxed and calm and never snaps at her kids (even if they are running late).

Janice

Janice is the class rep and a social butterfly. She loves socialising and is the first to volunteer to have everyone round to her house. She is a fantastic baker and always rustles up the best cakes for the cake stall at the summer fete. She makes the world's best chocolate fudge cake.

All four friends (!!) are very different, and this is where their beauty lies.

From this very simplistic example, we can see that each woman has a strength, something for which they are known, that sets them apart from everyone else. Do we ever see Rachel lamenting that she wishes she was more organised? Do we see Phoebe worrying that her outfit is last season's? Of course not! If Rachel had spent her time trying to be more like Monica, she would never have gone after her dream career in fashion.

So why, in the real world, do we stroll into the playground, see the lithe yoga bunny dressed in the latest Sweaty Betty attire and suddenly feel the urge to hotfoot it back home, log on to Amazon and buy a yoga mat? Two words: social influence.

Social influence has always been a thing, but it has become a much bigger thing since the rise of social media. Suddenly we have many more people on our radar: many more people to whom we are subconsciously comparing ourselves.

In order to prevent this overthinking and to stop the comparison that can eat away not only at our time, but also our headspace, we need to play to our strengths and not worry about what anyone else is doing. I have a wonderful friend who is much wiser than me when it comes to self-comparison. She always says, 'Keep your blinkers on.' If you keep your head down and just do your thing, you will progress towards your goals much faster. While everyone else is running around like headless chickens trying to be better at almost everything, you will be focused and moving forwards, towards where you truly want to go.

To put it simply: stay in your lane!

If we try and *be all of the things*, we will become confused about where we need to spend our time. We need to focus.

I think many of you will agree with me that it is much better to aim to be a master in your field, whether that is parenting, cooking, your career or getting out there and training for marathons. You are not superhuman (or Beyoncé) and this means that, no matter how much you try, hustle and grind, you will never be able to do it all. You will end up breaking yourself in two trying and you will feel utterly demotivated and stressed out.

It's much better to boss your bit of the planet and let the excess stuff fall naturally away. You will be far happier, and your brain will feel much clearer.

REMEMBER THE GOLDEN RULE: WE CAN BE ANYTHING WE WANT, BUT WE CANNOT BE EVERYTHING TO EVERYONE BECAUSE, QUITE SIMPLY, THERE ARE JUST NOT ENOUGH HOURS IN THE DAY.

Always wanting more and pushing too hard very often means that we miss what is going on in the present. If we look for it, we can see that there is beauty in the journey, and we should try to enjoy that.

Identifying your time-suckers will help you to be realistic about what you can achieve. Now, I'm not saying that you should give up on your hopes and dreams and throw your ambitions out of the window. Heck, if that was my attitude, I wouldn't be fulfilling my dream of writing a second book.

What I am telling you is that you need to find out what it is that is preventing you from reaching your goal, whether that goal is having a lie-in every Sunday, or becoming the top salesperson on your team. Going through the TOTT process will help you to free up the time you need to finally make your goal a reality. But not only that; it also will give you a realistic framework for how to get there.

4

The Time Cull – How to Claw Back Your Units

Those of you who have read my first book will know that I love a good clear-out. Culling clutter feels so satisfying, as it clears space for more important things in the home and does wonders for your mental clarity.

Well, do you know what feels just as satisfying as a clutter cull, if not more so?

A time cull!

This is where things start to get interesting. In the last chapter, we looked at the unhelpful thoughts, feelings and behaviours that are sucking away our valuable time. In this chapter, we're going to get more specific and look at the tasks and commitments that are either unnecessary or taking up more time than they should be.

Now that we are prioritising our time in the same way that we prioritise our hard-earned cash, seeing it as something that is not to be squandered or wasted, you will hopefully be starting to focus your mind, becoming able to understand which things matter most, and which things you can start to delete from your to-do list.

There are priorities that need your money's immediate attention when payday rolls around (your rent or mortgage, the household bills, etc.). The same applies to your time. Just as you wouldn't book a luxury weekend away before you had set money aside to pay your food bills, neither would you spend the morning languishing between the sheets if you needed to be at work two hours ago (or at least, I hope you wouldn't!).

Cash and time are very similar, and it will stand you in good stead to treat them both with the same reverence. However, there is one fundamental difference between the two.

Unlike cash, you can never get more time. No matter how hard you work or how much you grind, your daily budget of time will always be the same. This is a very sobering thought and is one of the great levellers in society. Time doesn't care about your social standing, how much money you have in the bank, how many holidays you have had this year or how many followers you have on Instagram. You can't save time for a rainy day; you can't bank it or multiply it through business deals. You use it or lose it.

Everyone has the same amount of time. And very often, it is how we spend that time that sets us apart from other people.

This means that we need to be savvy and we need to have a few tricks up our sleeves to make sure that we are using our time in the best possible way: a way that keeps us healthy, happy and fulfilled. Not in a way that makes us feel that we are on a never-ending treadmill of monotony, until our last day on earth.

Without this clarity, you will take on things that you do not really want to do (or that do not fit in with your priorities). You will waste your time and you will become resentful, spinning too many plates and *still* not achieving your goals.

If you know that, at the end of a long day, you only have one hour left over to play with (after all the necessary stuff like raising your kids, working and sleeping is done), it really brings into sharp focus that you cannot take on extra work for the PTA, or volunteer to be the class rep, yet again, because doing any of these things will take away from the little time you have left to yourself. (Yes, overachievers, I'm talking to you!)

It might sound selfish and ruthless but that really is the bottom line.

Again, look at time in the same way as you would cash. If you were down to your last £20 and you needed to buy food for the week, but you also saw your favourite boots were now available in brown, I am willing to bet you would prioritise you and your family being able to eat over buying yet another pair of boots. This is how it should be when it comes to the way you spend your time.

You have to be very realistic about how much time things *really* take. Majorly underestimating the amount of time you spend flicking through Instagram is just like sticking your head in the sand about how much you are spending on your credit card: you *will* come unstuck. The only person you are fooling is yourself (cough, spendthrifts, cough). Your time budget is being spent and you need to be honest with yourself about how you are spending it.

This is why it is absolutely crucial that we are honest during the Bootcamp process, because otherwise you will come away from it without a clear picture about the situation at hand. And this is why I was so insistent that you stuck with the Bootcamp process, rather than getting bored halfway through and leaving it unfinished (I hope you heeded my words of wisdom, dreamers!).

Now that you have properly gone through the Bootcamp process and you know how you are currently spending your time, you are in a fantastic position to start to rid your days of the dead wood. It's time to do a time cull.

THE CULL: HOW TO DECIDE WHAT MAKES THE CUT

This TOTT time cull is probably one of the most freeing exercises that you will ever do. Even better, as time goes by, you will be able to repeat this process again and again. You will start to become more efficient and ruthless in your culls because you will become more practised at being able to easily spot areas in your life that are not worth your time, enabling you to free up that time and spend it on something more important.

I want you to revisit your Bootcamp results and take a really good look at your notes. Now condense your notes into a clear list that sets out how you are spending your time on a typical day. Next to each entry, write down the amount of time it takes.

For example:

Going to the shops every day after work or the school run = two units each day.

By creating a clear factual list from your Bootcamp notes, you will see where you are wasting time. You won't be able to hide from it because it will be staring at you in black and white. You will start to see clear areas that you can change. Perhaps you could change to doing online weekly shops (or even monthly shops, if you have the space). This could save you two units each day: that's fourteen units a week and 728 units a year. That equates to a yearly time saving of 364 hours. That's fifteen days a year you are wasting on 'popping to the shop'. That is A LOT!

Starting to get the picture?

Think about what you could do if these units were repurposed and assigned to something more productive. When I say more productive, I don't mean I want you cramming yet more work into your day. It could be something lovely, like taking your kids to the park or spending those extra two units at the gym (and when I say gym, what I mean is relaxing in the sauna).

But what happens when you just can't decide what to keep in and what to get rid of? What happens when you are sitting, staring blankly at your units, thinking that you have twenty-eight hours' worth of stuff to fit into your twenty-four-hour day? If you don't know what to cull, you need to look at each thing on your list and ask yourself the following question.

What would happen if I didn't do it?

This simple, killer question is going to help focus not only your mind but also your priorities.

Let's look at a real-life example of a time cull in action.

Let's take a mum: let's call her Gemma. Gemma is a single mum and she is self-employed. She feels as though she has taken on far too much, and the stress and worry are starting to cause her sleepless nights.

Gemma has decided to give TOTT a go. After completing the Bootcamp process, she can see that she is indeed trying to do far too much (she has identified herself as an overachiever). The problem is, she doesn't know what to cull. She feels guilty that she is going to let people down and, if she is brutally honest with herself, this guilt is precisely the reason why she continues to take on too much. She worries that people will think badly of her or think that she is lazy if she doesn't look like super-mum to the outside world.

Gemma's list looks a bit like this.

- Caring for her elderly mum (she pops in daily on the way back from the school run).

- Running her business. Her business is fairly new, so she is doing everything for herself and learning as she goes along with things like tax returns, her website, etc.
- Helping at the school once a week, listening to children read.
- Doing all of the housework.
- Doing all of the cooking (plus making her son a packed lunch every day).
- Walking her dog daily.
- Doing the weekly food shop for both her and her mum every Saturday morning. She takes her mum with her so her mum can choose what she wants.
- Taking her son to football practice and matches every week.

OK. So that's what Gemma is faced with. She is just about managing to fit it all in (at a push), but she's left with hardly any time in the evenings for herself and she is starting to feel the strain on both her mental and physical health, especially during those weeks where she is feeling a little bit below par and is unable to operate at her normal fast pace, or when a spanner is thrown in the works by a sick child.

Gemma sits down with her list (which, now she has noted it all down in one place, has made it obvious to her why she has been struggling so much recently).

And now she applies the killer question: *what would happen if I didn't do it?*

Task	What would happen if she didn't do it?
Caring for her elderly mum (she pops in daily on the way back from the school run).	Her mum would feel lonely.
Running her business. Her business is fairly new, so she is doing everything for herself and learning as she goes along with things like tax returns, her website, etc.	She needs to run her business to keep food on the table and a roof over their heads.
Helping at the school once a week, listening to children read.	She would have to have a conversation with the school about it, but then she could stop right away. The worst-case scenario would be that it would cause minor inconvenience and maybe she'd feel some mum guilt.
Doing all of the housework.	The house would get messier.
Doing all of the cooking (plus making her son a packed lunch every day).	Her son needs feeding! As does she!
Walking the dog daily.	Rover would chew the sofa!
Doing the weekly food shop for both her and her mum every Saturday morning. She takes her mum with her so her mum can choose what she wants.	No one would eat.
Taking her son to football practice and matches every week.	He wouldn't get to go to football and he loves it.

Right, so we can see from this little exercise that Gemma can stop volunteering at the school with few to no consequences. While it might make her feel guilty in the short term, she needs to put herself first and knock that off the list, at least until she has more time available. Maybe in the future, when her business is running more smoothly, she can go back to helping out at the school.

But what about the rest? Is there anything Gemma can do in order to lighten the load a little bit?

Task	Can she approach this differently?
Doing all of the cooking (plus making her son a packed lunch every day).	Can she batch-cook using her slow cooker? Cooking twice the amount will take the same amount of time, and the extra portions can be popped in the freezer as homemade ready meals? Can she afford to pay for school dinners so that she doesn't have to make a packed lunch for her son every day?
Walking the dog daily.	Can she walk the dog after school? Or could she pay a dogwalker?
Doing the weekly food shop for both her and her mum every Saturday morning. She takes her mum with her so her mum can choose what she wants.	Could she go to her mum's house and place an online order to have her mum's shopping delivered? After the first few orders, her mum will have built up a list of favourites that would speed up the process even more. Gemma could order her own shopping at the same time. ▶

Task	Can she approach this differently?
Taking her son to football practice and matches every week.	Can she organise a carpool with some of the other parents from the team, so that they can take turns taking the kids to practice?

Let's delve a little bit deeper

When Gemma gets back home after doing the school run and popping in to see her mum, she immediately starts working on her business. During the school day, she also takes the dog out for a walk and she does her thirty minutes of TOMM. She eats her lunch at her desk because she wants to squeeze in as much work as she can while her son is at school.

Her business is doing well, and she is earning a good income, with next year set to be even better. But she is frustrated because she wants to grow her business faster. At the moment she is spending most of her time on the operational side of things: packing orders, dealing with customers, etc. She would like to spend more time on marketing and sales so that she can expand her business and ultimately earn more money.

Let's look at her units

Gemma gets home from the school run at 9.30 a.m. and needs to leave to collect her son at 3 p.m. This means that she has five and a half hours (eleven units) in the day to work on her business. Later on in the book, I'll show you how to further break down the day and assign units to various tasks to make your working day ultra-efficient, but for now let's see where we can claw back more time for Gemma to work on her marketing.

She is using two of her work units to do domestic tasks (walking the dog and completing her thirty minutes of TOMM). That's one hour of her working day that she could be using to grow her business – and spending one hour a day on marketing would be a great way to help her business grow.

This means that she has some options to consider.

- She could move her dog walk to after the afternoon school run. Maybe she can combine it with a trip to the park with her son.
- She could hire a virtual assistant to help with more of the operational tasks so that she can free up time to spend on marketing. This would be cost-effective if she were to bring in more revenue through the additional marketing than the VA would cost her.
- Her final option could be to hire a cleaner, freeing up an extra 30 minutes a day for marketing work. Again, this would only work if she were to bring in more revenue from the extra marketing than the cleaner would cost her.

Whoa! Hold on a minute there. What's this? Gemma Bray encouraging people to get someone else to do the cleaning for them?

OK, I am going to need you to bear with me on this one. I

know, *I know*. This seems like it is coming from way out of left field: after all, my first book was all about cleaning!

But as we can see from the example above, Gemma has successfully used TOMM to compartmentalise the cleaning into thirty minutes a day, and that allowed her to free up enough time to not only start her own business but also to push it forward, and now she is earning well from it. In fact, she is earning well enough that, if she rearranged her finances, she could afford a cleaner. It would make *good business sense* for her to free up her time in order to help her make even more money. So why isn't she already doing it? In short, because the idea makes her feel guilty. That's a big reason why lots of other women who could afford to hire a cleaner make the decision not to, because they feel that they *should* be doing it themselves, and that people will see it as lazy and indulgent. But right now, Gemma needs to read chapter nine (Guilt Gremlins), hire a cleaner and claw back some much-needed units, or she will remain stuck.

If she invested in a cleaner, the return on that investment would be two-fold.

- She would claw back more units, giving her more time.
- She would be able to use that time to market her business. This would bring in more money.

TOMM is an amazing tool for helping you to free up your time and stop the housework from leaking into most of your day. People are using this newly freed-up time in lots of different ways: some have started studying again, some have taken up new hobbies and others have started their own businesses. Now you can use TOTT to take things to the next level.

Levelling up is something to be proud of.

So it seems like the next, natural progression for Gemma would be to use the money that she has been able to earn by implementing TOMM to employ a cleaner and, potentially, a virtual assistant, which will then enable her to free up even more time (and headspace) and make more money!

This is how TOMM has ultimately helped me. At the beginning, I created it out of necessity. I was overcleaning, anxious and stressed following the birth of my first baby. Cleaning was taking up the majority of my day because I had convinced myself that if my house wasn't in immaculate condition all of the time, it somehow meant that I wasn't a good mum.

Luckily, I realised early on that my behaviour wasn't healthy and that I had to do something. I created TOMM and, out of that, TOTT grew. In the beginning, it gave me back time with my baby. As the years went on and my babies grew, I was able to use that time to start businesses. The first one was a successful antenatal business, and now TOTT has helped me to start a hugely successful blog from scratch, launch a social media career, develop a best-selling app and also write my first book, which was a *Sunday Times* Bestseller. TOTT helped me to do all of the above and is now helping me to find the time to write a second book.

'NO' IS A FULL SENTENCE: HOW TO SET BOUNDARIES

'Focusing is about saying "no".'
Steve Jobs

Pssst! Overachievers, you need this section!

Guarding your time carefully will inevitably mean having to say no to things you might previously have agreed to. This can be difficult, as you may feel you are letting other people down.

For a long time, I really struggled with saying no. In fact, I think it is something that will never come naturally to me. Over the years I have always done my best to avoid conflict. I often worried (too much) about what other people thought of me, meaning that I would put their opinions of me ahead of my own needs. I would say yes to things and agree to work on extra projects when I knew full well that I was already pushed for time. Because I was worried about 'causing a fuss' or looking lazy, I took the path of least resistance and just got on with it.

For years, I saw saying no or telling people that I didn't have time as a sign of weakness: a sign that I wasn't managing my time properly. I felt that, if I wasn't able to do everything that people asked of me, this meant that I was in some way a failure. The result? I would say yes to everything and carry on taking on more and responsibility, until eventually I would get sick or have a meltdown and end up crying into a glass of wine, telling my friends how I felt as though I was burned out.

Then I'd pull myself together (in the way that we are taught), pick myself up and force myself to start piling more stuff on to my shoulders.

This is not healthy and, in the long run, it is not productive. All that happens is that you risk burnout. When you are burned out, your body forces you to rest because it can't function properly, and you can't do anything at all.

Nowadays, saying no and being very strict with the number of things I take on is something that I constantly have to work at. It doesn't come naturally to me. I went to a high-achieving school where being a 'busy bee' was seen as a badge of honour: the busier we were, the more successful we were deemed to be, and the more extracurricular activities we had, the better!

It wasn't until I was older and running my own businesses that I realised how quickly you can become overwhelmed with the number of things that you are taking on, especially when you start to include looking after kids and maintaining a relationship.

I want you to look at it like this. For every additional, unnecessary thing that you take on, you are taking away time for doing something else.

When you agree to bake a cake for the class cake stall at the summer fete, you are agreeing to spend your time on that. If you are short on time already, you will have to find this time from somewhere else. Remember, you can't just pull extra time out of a hat.

If you have already allotted time to baking (because you

love it), you are on to a winner. But if you haven't, and you had been planning to spend the evening catching up with your other half over a glass of wine, a good meal and a movie, then you are faced with three options:

- Don't bake the cake and let someone at the school down.
- Bake the cake and let your other half down.
- Snog your other half's face off and buy the bloody cake from Marks & Spencer! Nobody will know or even care. For added authenticity, knock it about a bit and sprinkle on some icing sugar in a haphazard fashion before you drop it off.

And if anyone does say, 'This cake looks suspiciously like you bought it on the way to school this morning,' you can simply smile sweetly and reply, 'Yes, I did. I ran out of time for baking last night because I was having rampant sex with my boyfriend, so had to do the next best thing and buy it.'

Now obviously, it would have been much better if you had just said no (in a very polite, but very firm way) at the beginning. That would have saved all of this from having to happen (and perhaps spared a few blushes!). But it is all too easy to panic and say yes, just because you can't get the word 'no' into a sentence.

Here's the good news: 'No' is a full sentence on its own! No. See?

But if you want to have a few (more polite) ways to say no and help you guard your time, it's a good idea to have some stock sentences up your sleeve for 'saying no' emergencies.

Keep these in your arsenal:

- Thank you for asking me, but I don't have time to commit to anything else at the moment.
- I would have loved to, but my diary is full.
- I am sorry but I can't help you at the moment, I can't fit it in.

And, if you are in a true panic, use the good old:
I'll have to check my diary and get back to you.

This will give you some breathing space so that you can go home and work out a firm but polite way of declining. If you still don't want to say 'no' out loud, just send it in a text or email.

Now, if you have, up until now, spent most of your time blankly nodding along and agreeing to everything and anything that is asked of you, then the first few times you push back and say no you might well be met with a few puzzled looks. Just keep smiling and make sure that you stick to your guns.

Keep reminding yourself that, every time you take on an additional task, it will take time away from something else. This brings it into very stark focus. Visualise yourself not being able to have that oh-so-longed-for soak in a bubble bath while listening to your favourite podcast. That will make it much easier to say: 'No, Sandra. I can't sew the summer fete bunting by hand!'

HOW TO SAY NO AT WORK

Now, I know that some of you will be thinking, 'This is all well and good, Gem, but I can't tell my boss that I don't have time to do the work that he is asking me to do.'

I get that, in some cases, the hard line of 'I don't have time' just won't fly. And I get that it can be much harder for you to say no at work. After all, they are paying you for your time.

But what happens if your contract says that you're supposed to be working four days a week after you return from maternity leave, but you're doing five days' worth of work over those four days, plus you're staying later than anyone else, getting in earlier than anyone else, working through lunch *and* even taking some of your work home in the evenings and at the weekends just to try and keep on top of your emails?

If you have the sort of boss who, when you push back and say you don't have enough time, helpfully sends you on a time-management course rather than looking at your workload, you will need a better way of demonstrating that the fact you are not able to complete tasks is not down to a lack of skill or just laziness, but because you are being given too much work to do in the time you have.

There is a very subtle way of not only keeping your

workload manageable, but also showing your boss that you are unable to carry on working at the rate and pace that they are currently pushing for. And it is simply this:

I can't do X and Y at the same time. Which one would you like me to complete first?

5

Lightening the Load

If you find yourself facing the common conundrum of wondering how to get your partner on board then this chapter is for you. Of course, if you don't have a partner or if they are already pulling their weight then feel free to skip this bit and I'll see you in the next section.

Do you want to know why I do what I do? Do you want to know why I started talking about the ways in which people could compartmentalise their time so that they could give themselves more time to do other stuff? Do you want to know why I was willing to work pretty much full-time on a blog that didn't earn me more than £100 a month in the first year?

Well, I'll tell you. It is my true belief that there is more to life than the daily monotonous grind that goes hand in hand with being a grown-up. And it is also my true belief that women should not have to spend the majority of their adult life being the household's CEO. They should not bear the entire burden of running a home by themselves just because they are a woman.

I have been banging on about this for years (to anyone who will listen, in fact) via my podcast (*Life Laundry*, which I co-host with my dear friend and agent, Chippy), my YouTube channel, my blog and my other social media channels. If you have read my first book, you will know that it is the number-one message I put out there. All. The. Time. I feel that it is my mission in life to get the word out to as many people as possible.

I know how easy it is to fall into the trap of thinking that it would be quicker and easier if you just do everything yourself but, by doing this, you (either knowingly or unknowingly) become a martyr, sacrificing your own time (and life) so that your loved ones can go forth and live their lives unimpeded. This is doing yourself a massive disservice.

In the previous chapter, you carried out your time cull and looked at all the tasks in your daily and weekly routine that you could either eliminate, delegate or do more efficiently. This is a great first step, but if you feel that the overwhelming majority of the work involved in running your household falls to you, a time cull isn't going to be enough – you need to get your partner on board. Similarly, if you feel you are taking on too much because of an innate drive for perfection, or to match up to the lives you think everyone else is leading, you need to find a way to give yourself a break. This chapter is going to help you take these crucial steps towards clawing back your precious time.

If you feel that you are responsible for more than your fair share of the boring domestic stuff, it's important to address this with your other half and ask them to work with you to get some of your lost time back. This is probably something you have already discussed – or even argued about – on more than one occasion (don't they say that most couples argue about money and housework?), but if you're still in the same position, now is the time to make some changes.

Remember that you have bought this book to try and help you to manage your time better: to try to get off the hamster wheel of life where you get up, work, do the chores, go to sleep, get up, work, do the chores ... *ad infinitum*. But you can't do it without working as a team with your partner. By making TOTT work for you, you will both benefit by getting back some relaxation time that is guilt-free! So, with that in mind, let's look at what you can do to get an unwilling partner on side and stop being a martyr when it comes to running the household.

MARTYR NO MORE! WHAT TO DO WHEN OTHERS WON'T SHARE THE LOAD

This is such a tricky topic, but we can't skirt around it. To not address it would do a massive disservice to all the people who are struggling to divide up the workload at home. So, buckle up, folks: we're about to break it all down and get our hands dirty.

Before we get into this, I want to make it clear that this isn't me getting on my soapbox about men being lazy. I can think of several real-life cases where it is, in fact, the female in the relationship who isn't pulling her weight, leaving the man feeling hard done by and taken for granted. It can be so hard – and also bloody exhausting – to exist in a dynamic where you feel as though all of your efforts are not appreciated and that you are doing more than your fair share. And it can be even more frustrating when, despite having spoken to your other half about your concerns (many times!), nothing seems to be changing.

The resentment starts to creep into other aspects of your relationship, with things like your sex life starting to become affected. (Big hint: the average woman finds it hard to get into the sexy vibe when she's spent most of the evening tidying up with one eye on her other half while he seems oblivious to her efforts. There is nothing sexy *or* romantic about this scenario.)

When you dreamed about settling down with the love of your life, I'm willing to bet neither of you would have fantasised about having an argument over who was going to wash the Yorkshire pudding tray after Sunday dinner! But what can we do about it? Well, after years of talking to women who have similar problems (not just in TeamTOMM but friends in real life, too), I have come to the conclusion that it all boils down to one simple thing. Respect.

If you have spoken to your other half and calmly explained to them how it makes you feel when they don't pull their weight – that it makes you feel disrespected, undervalued and, if truth be told, a little bit unloved – and they are *still* not listening, the problem is going to be very hard to solve. Sorry, I know this probably isn't what you wanted to hear. As much as I would love to wave a magic wand over all of the households across the land and make the domestic division of labour equal, that is, sadly, not a skill I possess.

Now, let's be clear on this one. I am not telling you all to leave your partners because they haven't done the vacuuming. What I am suggesting you do is sit down and work out how much more you are doing than they are. Work out how much spare time you each have. Are they getting to do more fun stuff while you work away behind the scenes doing the laundry?

This is (again) a situation where you are going to need to be very honest with yourself. Because a few scenarios could be playing out here.

- Your other half is genuinely lazy and needs a kick up the backside.
- You and your other half have widely different expectations about how a house needs to be kept. They might have a much higher tolerance to mess, while you might start to feel stressed at the sight of a cushion being out of place.
- Your other half has no idea about the amount of work

you are doing behind the scenes and is oblivious to your passive-aggressive scrubbing of the lasagne dish on a Monday night.

- Perhaps *you* have no idea how much your other half is doing behind the scenes. They might be taking care of far more than you realise, while you are left assuming you are doing more than them. They might even feel that they are doing more than their fair share.

In each of these scenarios, the best thing to do is sit down and explain that you are not happy with the current situation and that you want – no, that you *need* – things to change, for the sake of your relationship and your happiness.

Obviously, this needs to be done in such a way that it doesn't end up in an argument, so timing and a calm approach are key. You need to demonstrate what it is that you are doing that is over and above what you believe to be your fair share. This is where going through the Bootcamp will come in handy, as you will have evidence of what it is you are doing with your time. If you can get your partner to do the Bootcamp at the same time as you, this will be an invaluable exercise because the evidence will be there in black and white for both of you. It will take away the '*I think*' and '*I feel*' part of the conversation, because the facts will be staring back at you. Hopefully this will be enough to redress the balance.

But if, even after sensible discussions, you have not got anywhere or, even worse, you feel as though you have been soothed with false platitudes or promises to change that will quickly be forgotten, then you are faced with a decision. Are you happy to carry on living the way you are, or are you able to cut down on the amount you are doing so that you don't feel so put upon?

Of course, there is a third, very tempting, option that I know most of us will have thought about doing at some point and that is to go on strike.

> 'I feel like going on strike for a week – they would soon see how much I do then!'

And, my word, it can feel tempting at times. Doing the housework, making the kids' dentist appointments, arranging play-dates, going to bloody soft-play for a party when you would rather stick pins in your eyes ... The mundane adult stuff that comes with running a home and having a family all adds up, and seemingly small tasks all combine to take up a lot of your time.

If I had £1 for every time we saw a post in the TeamTOMM Facebook group where the poster is at their wits' end and feels like a combination of a household maid, a PA and a chauffeur, I would be a rich woman. Very often they are at breaking point and are threatening to down tools and go on strike in a last-ditch attempt to shock the people they live with into finally paying attention to them and taking their struggles seriously.

The jury is always out on this sort of post, because this type of drastic action can be really hard to implement (and to keep up). You need to have nerves of steel as you willingly watch all of your hard work, the cumulative effect of your efforts over the months and years, come tumbling down as the house and family routines unravel around you.

It feels a bit like playing your fiddle while Rome burns.

Now, I have never personally taken this course of action. I have never downed my duster and gone on strike, because I know that I would be incapable of sitting on my hands and watching all of my hard work being undone around me. I am too much of a micromanager and I like things a certain way (I know, shocking, right?). I have no personal experience of a mum strike, but I know that plenty of women in my TOMM community have tried it, so I asked them what the upshot was. Here is what they told me:

'It failed miserably, and I ended up having mountains of cleaning to do. Total own goal.'

'I did it for four weeks and it killed me! Eventually nobody helped, so I just got on with it – but shouted about it the entire time.'

'I did it years ago. It made a point at the time and they were good for a couple of weeks, but it didn't last, unfortunately!'

'It doesn't work. It just pissed everyone else off, too. I think anything passive aggressive like that should be avoided. It's also REALLY easy to get bogged down in our own viewpoint and story that we replay in our heads. That's the most damaging thing, in my opinion.'

There's a bit of a theme developing here, isn't there?

More than two hundred people replied, and I can tell you that the vast majority of them said going on strike does not work. And I think the final person quoted above makes a really good point: if things get so bad that you feel as though you have to play games in order to get something to change, then there has been a massive communication breakdown. If you can talk about it, please keep trying; it is a much healthier approach.

TRY LEAVING THIS PAGE LYING OPEN FOR YOUR OTHER HALF TO READ (JUST IN CASE)

I think your other half would like to work with you on something. It's important to them that you read this small section of the book. Don't worry, I will keep it brief.

There is a very good chance that your other half feels as though they are doing more than their fair share of the boring domestic stuff. Maybe they have spoken to you about it before, or maybe the two of you have argued about it on more than one occasion.

▶

Your partner bought this book so that they can try to manage their time better. They want to try to get off the hamster wheel of life where they get up, work, do the chores, go to sleep, get up, work, do the chores ... you get the picture.

I have written a whole book to help them to achieve this, but they can't do it without you working with them as a team. When they talk to you about it, please be open-minded. This could be the start of some really positive changes for the pair of you, both individually and as a partnership.

The aim of this book is to give you *both* back some much-needed relaxation time that is *guilt-free*! So please, give it a try. It could be the start of something amazing!

THINK ABOUT WHAT'S REALLY WORTH YOUR TIME – AND GIVE YOURSELF A BREAK

Often, it isn't an unsupportive partner that's the problem. It's ourselves. As women, we can sometimes be our own worst enemies. Not only do we feed our obsession for perfection and constant self-improvement by scrolling through our social media feeds and staring longingly at the gorgeous homes we see there (ideals that, for many us, are impossible to achieve); we then turn the glare on ourselves and wonder why it is that *we* haven't got all of the lovely cushions, immaculate kitchens and Caribbean holidays that we see on social media. It leaves us with a constant feeling of never quite being satisfied.

We talked earlier about the danger of the comparison culture we live in and the way it sucks away our time. I believe that the main reason we feel drawn to such portrayals of perfection is because it is human nature to have something to aspire to. Inspirational images of 'ideal' lifestyles can motivate us to strive for better in our own lives.

On the one hand, this motivation can be a healthy thing, but when you take it too far, it can have a damaging (sometimes catastrophic) effect on your state of mind and wellbeing. It is all well and good being inspired to spend £30 on a new set of dinner plates that have been co-designed by your favourite blogger, but this can quickly spiral out of control when you are left feeling miserable that you can't afford to replace your entire kitchen to reflect the current trend that is sweeping your socials.

We know comparison is the thief of joy, but comparison can steal our time, too.

It can do this by enticing us to spend our time mindlessly scrolling through social media, but it can also take up your time (and your headspace) in other ways, as you are left subconsciously pondering why you have been left with the short straw compared to the people who seem to constantly be on holidays and nights out, with seemingly endless pots of cash to buy new stuff every day.

So, you work even harder, pushing yourself to the limit to achieve it. Here's the thing: even if you work yourself to the bone, save up for years and mortgage yourself to the hilt so that you can buy your dream house, somebody still needs to put in all the hard work to make sure that the house looks perfect twenty-four seven. And, if you are the only one who can be bothered to chase that image of perfection, then guess what? Yes, that's right: it will fall on *your* shoulders, and you will be using *your* precious time units to make it happen.

If you enjoy doing it, and you genuinely don't mind spending your time units on keeping house and running the home like some sort of well-planned military operation, then you are on to a winner. But if you don't, you will soon start to feel more than a little miffed.

THIS ISN'T THE GIRL GUIDES – THERE'S NO MARTYR BADGE

If you are keeping your home to someone else's standards, be they Instagram ideals or some romantic vision that belongs in a glossy magazine, then you are going to start martyring yourself for a cause that is, to be blunt, not worth it.

You might start out full of vim and vigour, working your socks off trying to create the dream lifestyle for you and your family, proud of the home environment that you are lovingly curating. Hell, you might even be receiving praise from your friends when they visit (and even your family, who are enjoying the fruits of your labours). But, pretty soon, you will start to sniff out the imbalance and you will become very aware that the pleasure–pain ratio is not working in your favour. You're taking on all of the pain, while they are enjoying all of the pleasure. You're doing most of the work, while others are enjoying the rewards.

If you've ever passively aggressively washed up the dinner dishes while your other half sits back and turns on the TV, you will know exactly what I am talking about.

At this point some of us will naturally think, 'Stuff this! I'm going to sit down, too.'

But others – and these are the people who are most vulnerable to falling into the trap of martyrdom – will grit their teeth and get on with the dishes.

These are the people who need TOTT to come to the rescue. If you stick to your TOTT plan, running your home doesn't have to take over your life. You will keep the housework, the life admin and everything else that comes with being a grown-up in its box, so that you can still be you and not feel like a slave to the house.

6

How to Make TOTT Your Own

Welcome to the part of the book that you have all been waiting for. And welcome to the first day of the rest of your life! Tad dramatic? Maybe ... but I truly believe that your life is going to get *a hell of a lot easier* once you have put TOTT in place.

This is where you will start to make changes and you will, very quickly, begin to see the positive impact that TOTT can have. You have been through Bootcamp, you have been ruthless and culled all of the dead wood; now is the time to start planting the seeds for your new way of organising your time.

Are you ready?

LET'S GET DOWN TO BUSINESS

As I've already explained, your TOTT day is going to be divided into a series of thirty-minute chunks: that's forty-eight units.

Let's start with a blank day: a blank canvas of forty-eight units.

TOTT, just like TOMM, divides jobs into three levels.

Level-one jobs: things that absolutely have to get done ... or the shit will hit the fan!

This is where you need to allocate your time first, as these are your non-negotiables. These are things that you need to do every day, to keep yourself and your dependants healthy. I want you to include things like:

- sleeping
- bathing/showering
- eating, making sure you and your kids are nourished
- caring for an elderly relative

Level-two jobs: things that are important, but can wait or be postponed if needs be

These are the things that are not life-and-death, but that would cause major disruption if you were to not get them done regularly enough.

- work (I know that, to many of us, work is vital and you might think it should be in level one, but my

reasoning for putting it at level two is that, if you *really* need to, you can take a day off sick)
- getting the kids to school
- doing your tax return
- cleaning your house, doing laundry, etc.

Level-three jobs: focus tasks

These are the things that you always *want* to get around to doing, but never quite manage to fit in. This is where you start to make the time. Cue chorus of angels!

- having a bath
- taking up that new hobby that you've been wanting to try for years
- reading a book
- setting up a side business
- writing a book!

PUTTING IT TOGETHER

Now, I know you all want to skip to the good bit (I totally get it!). I know that you want to jump straight to the part where you decide what you are going to do with your level-three time, but you can't do that until you work out how much level-three time you have!

If you jump into deciding what you want to do with your level-three time, you will be setting up your TOTT plan backwards. This means things won't work and the system will break down. Before we plan in our level threes, we must make sure we are making time for the necessary (and maybe slightly boring) jobs on levels one and two.

For those of you who love a good visualisation, think of your level-one and level-two jobs as the legs of the swan working hard under the surface, while the level threes will make it appear that you are effortlessly gliding to three hot yoga sessions a week.

Remember: you have already done the culling exercise in chapter four, so all the jobs that remain for levels one and two absolutely have to be there.

First things first: cementing in those level ones

Your level-one jobs are like the scaffolding that will hold up the rest of your TOTT plan and, if we are going to continue that dramatic theme, your life! Work out how much time you are going to be spending on your level-one jobs and get them firmly cemented in your day.

Remember these are non-negotiable, and they can't be moved.

For example, if you have listed sleep as one of your level ones and someone tries to schedule something in during your sleep time (perhaps your boss has asked you to come in an hour early for a meeting, meaning you have to get up an hour earlier) and you are not able to drag and drop your level ones to elsewhere in the day (for example, by moving your units around so you can get to sleep an hour earlier the night before), then you have to be brutally honest and tell whoever is making the request that you do not have time and that you will schedule it in for another date.

This is really important. There is no point putting time and effort into TOTT if you are not prepared to guard the time like your life depends on it. And, to be frank, a part of your life does depend on it – the fun part!

When you put in your level ones, please do not be shocked at how much time they take up. Just take a breath and move on to adding in your level twos.

Second things second: let's add in those level twos

Again, these should be fairly static. Get them sealed into your TOTT plan and see how many units they require.

Now bring in the level threes

Now we can work out how much time you have left for the oh-so-longed-for level-three treats!

If you are a nine-to-five, Monday-to-Friday worker, you may find that your typical weekday looks like this once you've assigned all your level-one and level-two jobs:

- Sleep: 16 units (level 1)
- Work: 12 units (level 2)
- Housework: 1.5 units (if you are following TOMM) (level 2)
- Getting yourself and the kids ready in the morning: 4 units (level 1) (having breakfast is included in this)

- School run/commute: 2 units (level 2)
- School pick-up/home commute: 2 units (level 2)
- Dinner prep and evening meal: 4 units (level 1)
- Bath/bedtime with kids: 2 units (level 2)

Total: 43.5 units.

This leaves you with 4.5 units for your level-three 'me time'. That's two hours and fifteen minutes, which is a pretty decent chunk of time, don't you think?

But what happens when all of this time doesn't come packaged up in neat consecutive units? Having ten minutes here and there isn't much use if your aim is to have a long soak in the bath! Here are a few ways to be savvy with other parts of your day so you can free up time for those very precious level threes. Hopefully these suggestions will get you thinking about other ways you can be more efficient and pretty soon you'll be freeing up time like a pro.

- Instead of sitting through the TV adverts staring blankly into space while someone tells you about another sofa sale, get up and do a quick five-minute job. This could be emptying or re-loading the dishwasher or folding some washing.
- While you are waiting for the kettle to boil, have a quick wipe down of your kitchen counters. Keeping on top of this throughout the day will save the monumental clean-up after dinner time (leaving you more time for that bath).

- When cooking dinner, make double the amount to keep in the freezer for another time. You will have spent the same amount of time (and effort) cooking, but you will have created a meal for a dinner in the future. Hey presto! A time win.

NOW COMES THE FUN PART!

This is the part where you get to choose what you do with your free time. Usually, this is where a mild panic can set in. If you are used to operating at top speed, going through life just turning the cogs, ticking things off and never actually feeling as though you are doing anything fun, being suddenly faced with free time can actually be a little daunting (and perhaps a bit emotional).

You might be sitting at your kitchen table right now, suddenly faced with the strange notion that you have some spare time, but you don't actually know what to do with it. This is perfectly normal, especially if you have been stuck on the hamster wheel for a while and you have forgotten what it is like to have a life that exists outside of work and parenthood.

I know that we all fantasise about what we would do if we could have even five minutes to ourselves, but often when we are actually given some glorious free time, the sheer number of possibilities can blind and overwhelm us, and we end up baffled by all of the available options. Part of you might really want to get in a bath and listen to a podcast, while another part of you wants to join the local gym and make use of their free Pilates classes.

It is perfectly normal to realise, at this point, that you have slowly chipped away at your hobbies over the years in order to make way for jobs and chores until there is nothing left. It can make you quite emotional and, if truth be told, a little bit sad. You will have undoubtedly taken what seemed to be your only option at the time, which was to sacrifice the non-essentials, so that you could keep your head above water and get everything done. The things that people sacrifice first are often their own hobbies, and any free time that they have quickly gets eroded. This is because they can't justify the time being spent on what they see to be 'frivolous' activities, like self-care, when there are more important things that need to be done, like adulting, paying the gas bill, picking Tom and Jonny up from swimming lessons or taking the empty bottles to the bottle bank. If you are faced with choosing between taking a bath or doing the grocery shopping (because you don't have time to do both) the grown-up in you will pull up your socks and bring home the bacon (literally). Very often, we sacrifice what we *want* to do in order to do what *needs* to get done.

But now that you have got TOTT in your life, you will have made room for all of the necessary jobs while leaving yourself some guilt-free time. BOOOM!!

And we haven't even touched on the weekends yet!

If you are already following TOMM, you will know that weekends are purposefully kept housework-free, meaning that the weekend doesn't have to be one mammoth housework catch-up session. TOMM allows you to keep the weekends for the fun stuff. If you work a Monday-to-Friday job, boy, oh boy, are you going to have some fun planning your TOTT plan for the weekend! Because (if you are following TOMM) not only will you have no housework to do, but you will also have planned your week in such a way that the level-three time that you factor in for Saturday and Sunday will be gloriously guilt-free. Of course, not everyone works a typical week. Some of you will work shifts; some of you will have days off in the week. Either way, the time that is meant for pleasure can stay that way when you use TOTT.

The beauty of TOTT is that it doesn't have to look the same from day to day and week to week. Unlike your level ones and level twos, the lovely, lovely level threes do not have to be static. You can change them daily, weekly or monthly: as often as the mood takes you. They are there to serve your every whim and fancy.

You might even decide to just use them to go to bed early – or maybe, just maybe, if you work from home, to take a nap or a bath in the middle of the day.

I have never done this.

(I totally have.)

Your level threes are guilt-free because you know that you have already taken care of the essentials. So, not only will you be able to have some 'me time', you will also have the headspace to fully enjoy it and embrace it, without being plagued by guilt that you could or should be doing something more worthwhile.

It might feel a little bit strange at first but remember that you have already allowed the time for the important stuff in life with your level ones and level twos. What's more, you know that the time that you have set aside for all the important stuff is realistic, because you timed it all when you went through Bootcamp!

You might find yourself feeling a bit emotional (or, dare I say it, ashamed) about the fact that you had let life get in the way of you being able to do the things you love. Please don't be so hard on yourself. You haven't let yourself down; you did what needed to be done at the time. The good news is you now have lots of time to explore what you enjoy and get to know yourself again.

It can be really easy to lose yourself in parenthood. It happens to all of us at times. But, with TOTT on your side, it doesn't have to be that way. I promise you that being able to look at your free time as guilt-free is an absolute game-changer.

THE IMPORTANCE OF BEING FLUID WITH YOUR BUDGET

At the time of writing, as I mentioned earlier, we are in the midst of the Covid-19 pandemic. The situation in which we have found ourselves across the world has made it very clear that life sometimes likes to throw a spanner in the works, and that occasionally we have to learn to just go with the flow. We can be coasting along quite happily in a routine when – boom! Everything feels as though it has been flung up in the air and we are left scrambling to get our lives back under control again.

Sometimes the saying 'Life is what happens when you are busy making other plans' rings one hundred per cent true. We must learn to navigate life's twists and turns.

Recognising that TOTT is not a prescriptive plan is *key*. We need to move with the push and pull, not only of our lives, but also of our days. Things happen and that's OK. Getting stressed about a change of plan will just make it even harder for you to get back on track.

Let's say you had planned to spend four units going out to lunch with a friend, but life happens and instead you have to go and collect a poorly child from school. This has the potential to unravel the rest of your day, not only meaning that you miss your much longed-for catch-up with your friend, but also that any work you had planned for the rest of the day will have to be put on hold.

Let's explore how to safeguard against that and why it is important to always have a contingency plan (in case of a poo-nami or a sick kid).

The most important way to safeguard your time from unexpected events is to plan your whole week in advance and make sure that you factor in some contingency time. I always try to do my planning on a Sunday. For most of us this won't take too long, as most of our weeks will look largely the same thanks to work, school and the other regular, structured activities that make up our level ones and level twos. But you should never just assume that each week will be the same: don't get complacent! Just as doing regular Time Bootcamps will help to keep your life on track, so will taking a little time before the start of each week to make sure that you aren't going to be caught on the hop by something like World Book Day! Planning the week ahead will help you to do two things.

- It will help you to get a bird's eye view of the upcoming week, enabling you to give it a quick scan to make sure that you are using your units as efficiently as possible.
- If you are faced with an unexpected event, you will be able to quickly see which units you can move around to try to cover the problem. Think of it like a virtual 'drag and drop'. Having the whole week already planned out will make this much easier.

If you have been sticking to TOTT for a while, you will notice that, as time passes (because you have been using time efficiently), unexpected events, while annoying, do not have the same catastrophic effect as they used to.

In your pre-TOTT days, you might have left a work project until the last minute, only to come down with a bad cold the day before the deadline. This might have put you firmly in panic mode, struck by the fear that you were going to have to rush to complete the project while not feeling great. Not a good recipe for doing your best work.

Now that you are following TOTT, leaving things to the

last minute will become a thing of the past and you will be in a much better place to take life's twists and turns in your stride.

Planning some contingency into your days is a great method of safeguarding against some of the smaller ways in which life can get in the way of your plans. For example, you could add a quarter of a unit on to your commute in case there is traffic, or your train is delayed. Remember: contingency is essential.

Obviously, we can't plan for every eventuality, but having a TOTT plan that is too rigid and has no wriggle room will mean that, when something does happen that isn't accounted for in your day, it could have the potential to bring the rest of your week down with it. Plan in some time buffers to stop the carnage leaking into any more time than is absolutely necessary.

How to stop the spread of a day gone wrong

It is inevitable that we will come across days where the universe seems to be conspiring against us and we can't seem to get anything running according to our plan. But how do we make sure that times like this are just a blip and that they don't leak into the rest of the day or week?

- You have to accept some collateral damage. If you can, try to write off the lost time. If it wasn't a crucial level-one or level-two job, just let it go. Yes, it might suck that you didn't get to go to Zumba because your car broke down but, unless you can fit it into some level-three time elsewhere in your week, just take a deep breath and move on.

- If it is a crucial job, like getting a piece of work finished on time, then you need to take a bird's-eye view of your week. Look at the week as a whole: can you switch anything around? Are there any work tasks that you have planned for later in the week that you can postpone until next week? This would enable you to claw back some time so that you can meet your deadline.

- Where possible, always try to claw back lost time from units that belong in the same level. Only in an absolute time emergency should you be eating into your level threes to claw back time lost on level ones or level twos. Remember, the key to TOTT is balance. The whole reason we are guarding our level threes so ferociously is because we want you to get off the hamster wheel of life.

7

How to Stay on Track

Making a big change in your life isn't an easy thing to do. By creating your own TOTT plan, you have completely reassessed the way you have been spending your time up to now and decided to do things differently. It's hugely empowering, but it can also be overwhelming, and there are many internal and external factors that will come along and threaten to blow you off course. In the following chapters, we're going to look at the deep-seated beliefs that threaten to hold you back from fully embracing TOTT: things like 'mum guilt' and not feeling like you're worthy of self-care. We're also going to look at external forces that might cause you to stop following your TOTT plan, such as other people's expectations or lifestyle factors, like sleep deprivation. Some of these sections may be a hard read for some of you, but it's big-girl-pants time. If you don't address these issues, TOTT is very unlikely to work for you in the long run.

BEWARE OF ENTITLEMENT: BOTH THEIRS AND YOURS!

First, let's talk entitlement. We're going to start with your own entitlement and how it can throw a major spanner in the works by skewing your perspective about time.

Time doesn't owe you anything

Are you guilty of looking around and seeing people getting their nails done, spending an hour a day in the gym or going away for weekends and wondering why the hell you aren't able to do the same?

This can be a very bitter pill to swallow, especially if you feel as though you are constantly working your bum off. Maybe you are genuinely baffled as to where other people find all of this spare time. Maybe you are studying for a qualification that will allow you to get your dream job, or maybe you have just started your own business and most of your time is taken up with hustling to get it off the ground. It can be really hard not to feel resentful when you see others having a jolly good time with their level threes when you are busting your buttons using yours to try to get ahead and make your life better.

Take a deep breath. Remind yourself that you have been

through Bootcamp. That means that every task you have been left with is necessary and needs to be there in order for your life to run smoothly. These are the cards that you have been dealt. I know it sounds harsh, but it's true. We can only work with what we have.

It will do you no favours to press your face up against the window of someone else's life. You are only ever seeing a snapshot, not the full picture. You don't know what is going on for them behind closed doors. They could be burning the midnight oil and working through the night for all you know. Very often people only show you what they want you to see. And isn't that the truth with social media? Social media is one of the worst things for making us feel hard done by, as we watch people live a life that seems much more fun than ours.

Remember the saying: 'Don't compare your behind-the-scenes with someone else's highlight reel.' (Dreamers and overachievers in particular can be very guilty of losing focus because of this.)

You cannot compare your situation with someone else's, because no two people's situations are the same. It's a totally unfair comparison. Everyone (and I mean everyone) has the same number of units in the day. What sets people apart is how they choose to use their time. How they spread their tasks across the day is up to them. This does not only apply to how they are using their units *today*, but also how they chose to use their time *yesterday* and all of the days before that.

Let me explain what I mean.

Everyone you meet or observe will have been on their own

journey to get to where they are. Any success or spare time that they are enjoying now might be a direct consequence of how they chose to spend their time in the past. Maybe the person who is at the gym for an hour a day has been building up their business over the years and is now reaping the rewards. Maybe now they are able to afford to pay someone to help lighten the load and take on some of the tasks that they are not naturally good at (and so were spending far too much time on). Maybe they are now repurposing the units they have saved to help them look after their mental and physical wellbeing.

We are all responsible for our own time, just like we are all responsible for our own money. Everyone has very different priorities that dictate how they spend both.

The reality is that, if you have eight units left and you need to work (to pay the bills), but you also want to go to the spa and get your nails done, there has to be a moment where you become accountable to yourself. Just because someone else is doing it, doesn't mean that you are automatically entitled to do the same.

You can't stamp your feet and say it's not fair, stubbornly go and get your nails done and then complain that you never have enough time to get your work done. You have to be realistic. Because the reality is that you did have time, but you chose to spend it on your nails.

Trust in the process and know that the work and the time you are putting in now will pay off later. You are investing your time. The person you are envious of might have cashed in their past investments and may now be enjoying the fruits of their labour.

And always remember to use your units as you intended (spendthrifts, I'm talking to you!). If you do, then you will have the chance for some downtime, too. If you waste your units, you will end up regretting it. Falling into a scroll-hole or losing time on a YouTube binge will eat into the time that you had planned to do something else. And if you're watching cat videos on YouTube instead of cracking on with your work, guess what? You've just turned your level-two time into level-three time, and that means you'll have to claw back those lost units from your precious level threes.

You don't owe anyone your time

Now that that's out of the way, let's look at how other people might lean on you and feel as though they are entitled to some of your precious time in order to make their own lives easier.

Picture the scene: you have just sat down to enjoy your two units of peace and quiet reading a book on a sunny Sunday afternoon in the garden, when all of a sudden, out of nowhere, your other half spots that you 'aren't doing anything' and asks you to help them put the washing on the line. They can see that you look more than a little unkeen to pitch in, so they pull out that old favourite one-liner: 'Oh, come on. It'll only take ten minutes.'

Let me tell you a story about a real-life situation that would often happen to me when I was running my own fish-and-chip shop. Running a chippy was, by far, one of the hardest jobs I have ever done. It is tiring (I was on my feet for twelve hours a day with very little rest), and smelly, the clean-up is a greasy nightmare and you work really unsociable hours.

We used to close at 9.30 p.m. as I didn't want to be open when the pubs kicked out. Now, all of the locals *knew* what time we closed, but that didn't stop people trying their luck and coming in at 9.28 p.m., expecting you to cook them cod, chips and peas for four people because, yes, you've guessed it . . .

'Oh, come on. It'll only take five minutes!'

Now this is true: it would only take five minutes. But what would happen if someone else saw that we were still cooking at 9.30 p.m. and decided to try their luck too? That's another five minutes – and so on and so forth. Before I knew it, I could have another six people in the queue, meaning I was working for thirty minutes more than I wanted to.

The direct result of the entitlement of others meant that I was losing my very precious downtime. I used to get home at 11 p.m. each night because of how long it took to clean up. If I had given my time away, I would find myself scrubbing the kitchen thinking about how I was probably too tired now to stay up and enjoy my half-hour ritual of watching *Friends* before bed. I had sacrificed my downtime because someone else couldn't manage to order their food on time.

So, I started to guard my time ferociously. I learned to say no. And guess what? The customers learned to get their bums to the chippy on time.

Boundaries and respect are your secret weapons here. I was known to quickly pull the roller shutters down as repeat offenders made their way across the car park.

Never be afraid to stand your ground.

Beware the Time Cuckoo

Remember: it's of crucial importance to hold firm on your time boundaries (think back to all that effort you put into your time cull in order to free up these precious units in the first place).

When your colleagues or the eagle-eyed people in the PTA (joke – I love the PTA, they do a fine job and I have been a member in the past, when I had time!) start cottoning on to the fact that you are suddenly a lot more chilled out, they might start to helpfully try to fill up your time again. How generous of them!

Someone might spot that you are no longer staying late at work; instead you are clocking off at a reasonable time and are on your way to have dinner with your dad. To the time-poor, this will not go down well. You must be on your guard from incoming attempts at sabotage.

You need to be especially wary of Time Cuckoos. They will try to steal your new little nest egg of time and take it for themselves.

Even if you are not vocal about your new way of doing things, Time Cuckoos will see that you are off doing nice things with your level threes and, for one reason or another (probably because they feel stressed out), they will take exception to this and try to use up your time so that they can lighten their own load.

This is something that you have to keep a keen watch for, especially in the workplace, for it is a very slippery slope. Now, I am not saying you should never help a colleague in need. What I am saying is that you should be watchful for the ones who will take the proverbial, because there is always one – and, if truth be told, you probably already know who they are.

You know how it starts.

'Ooh, you couldn't do me a massive favour, could you? While you're sitting drinking that coffee, can you just run your eye over this report and make a few changes?'

You agree and, before you know it, you are the unofficial office proofreader.

'Just give it to Gem, she's fab at that sort of stuff!'

Bang: some of your hard-won units have gone up in smoke.

Some people will do this because they begrudge you the time to yourself, jealous that you are holding it all together better than they are. Others will do it simply because they are drowning under the weight of their own jobs and they genuinely need help. These are the people who need to know about TOTT. (Don't tell the mean ones about it though; they can suffer.)

Joking!

(I'm not.)

8

Breaking Old Habits and Creating New Ones

I mentioned in the previous chapter that making big changes can be a huge challenge, and there is no part of this that's more difficult than changing your mindset and subconscious beliefs about the way you need to approach your life after you become a parent. But changing this mindset and these beliefs is exactly what TOTT is asking you to do.

I noticed (and maybe you did too) that after I became a mum, I started to operate on some sort of mum-turbo light speed whenever I was doing anything for myself: you know, like having the audacity to take a shower that was more than three minutes long.

I always had the thought in the back of my mind that my

baby was going to need me or that, as soon as I dipped my toe into the water of a much longed-for bath that someone, somewhere would shout, 'Muuuuum? Mum! MUMMY!!' The result was that I never fully relaxed, meaning that I was never really getting any true pleasure from even the small acts of self-care that I managed to shoehorn into my day.

I know that I am not alone in this. And this means many of us never truly relax or really feel that we are allowed to take pleasure in something that takes us away from our parental duties.

It sometimes feels like, once we become a parent, our ability to prioritise ourselves is surgically removed, along with the placenta. The bit of our brain that allows us to truly relax and enjoy ourselves independently of our children seems to pack a bag and move out. How many times have you paid for a babysitter to enable you to go out for a much-anticipated meal with your other half, only to spend most of the evening checking your phone or texting to make sure that everything is OK back at home?

We've all done it. It comes with the territory of being a parent. It just becomes instinct.

Believe me: I truly, hand on heart, understand that, for a lot of you, getting into the habit of putting yourself first, even for a small part of your day, is going to feel really bloody weird. I think it's something that we have to work at and constantly remind ourselves to do. I know that I have to take myself to task from time to time and have a word with myself if I see that my self-care is slipping. And when I say put yourself first, I really do mean *put yourself first*. Do something that completely takes you away from the parenting world. Try to take yourself out of the house, so you can't hear little voices squabbling over whose turn it is on the PlayStation. If that isn't possible, make sure that your level threes are planned in for after the kids are safely in bed.

For each of us, what we choose to do with our level-three units will be different. It will depend on the number of level-three units we have, the cash we have available and also the stage of life we are at. A new mum's level threes are going to look *very* different to those of a mum who has kids that are all away at university.

I recently I revisited my level threes – and I levelled up. This took the form of me rethinking my finances in order to free up the money to enable me to join a gym that had a spa. I looked at my direct debits and got rid of the things that were not as important to me as my self-care. This was a huge deal for me. *Huge*. Massive!

I grew up in a working-class family and my parents are some of the hardest-working people I know. While I was growing up, it was drummed into me that hard work meant results and that laziness was something that was looked down upon. When I decided to join that gym, I had to really fight the hardwiring within me that was trying to convince me not to do something that was going to benefit my mental health. I had to fight against my upbringing, which was screaming at me that the right thing to do would be to continue to work at top speed and deal with the consequences later.

I don't think it ever gets easier. It's almost as though we are constantly battling the 'mum guilt' on a basic, instinctive level, and I really struggled to join that gym. I went in three times to have a look around before I finally bit the bullet.

How crazy is that?

And I have a confession to make. I hid the fact that I was going to a gym that had a spa from most of the people I knew. For a while, I didn't talk about it on my social media channels. Why?

I felt guilty and I was worried that people would judge me or think I was some sort of lazy lady of leisure (there's that fear of being labelled as lazy rearing its head again!). The more I agonised over it, the more it became clear to me that this was *absolutely* something that had to be spoken about. Because if we don't talk about it, and if we don't celebrate the moments of self-care that we have carved into our lives, things will never change.

So, repeat after me:

SELF-CARE IS NOT SELFISH.

RELAXING IS NOT A WASTE OF TIME

How sad is it that, as women and mums, we feel so bad about treating ourselves with the same love and care that we lavish on our loved ones that we actively berate ourselves if we decide to take a break and go and sit in a sauna for fifteen minutes at the end of our workout? I was working in excess of fifty hours week, so was not in any way lazy (*there I go again, still trying to justify myself*) but I still felt as though I was somehow not entitled to take time for myself to relax.

Before TOTT, I would try to cram as much into my day as I could, squeezing every last productive minute out of it to try to be the ultimate super-mum. I went through periods of crippling anxiety because my adrenaline was through the roof, but I carried on pushing forwards, navigating through my days at one hundred miles an hour.

Even after I developed TOTT, there were times when I was not using it wisely. I was merely using it as a way to be as efficient as possible, basically turning myself into a machine. Inevitably, that machine broke down. This is why it is vital that you make yourself do regular Time Bootcamps: I suggest doing at least two a year. This will make sure that you catch yourself before you fall back into the trap of taking on more and more. Don't assume that one Bootcamp will do it. It is very easy for old habits to creep back in. You need to be careful and continue to prioritise your own health as much as you prioritise everyone else's.

When I finally joined that gym, it was after a period where I had been misusing TOTT to fit in as much work as I could. I was exhausted, and my body was forcing me to rest. I would be able to keep up the momentum for a few weeks, then I would burn out, rest for a bit and pick myself up and start over – only for the cycle to repeat itself, again and again, and again.

At last, I realised that something had to change. As my mum always says, 'If you don't change the way you do things, everything will stay the same.'

It became clear to me that there was an imbalance between the amount of time I was spending on working and the time I was spending on myself. I decided that it was time to do a new Time Bootcamp and a fresh cull. When I wrote down how much I was trying to achieve, I was blown away that I hadn't realised it sooner. But, as we all know, sometimes we just can't see the wood for the trees.

If you start to feel like this, just remember the bucket visualisation from chapter two. Doing regular Bootcamps will make sure that you are keeping your bucket in tip-top condition and enable you to plug up any holes before they start to become too much of an issue.

MOTHERING THE MOTHER

When I was an antenatal teacher and doula, there was a phrase that we would use a lot: 'Mother the mother'.

This is something that is *so* important, but often gets neglected. As a mum, you often find yourself running around trying to make everything run smoothly for everyone else, looking after all of your loved ones. But who is looking after *you*?

The stark reality that many of us face is that, if we do not look after ourselves, nobody else will. Nobody else is going to make sure that we are tucked up in bed by a reasonable hour, with brushed teeth and a belly full of comforting food. It is down to us.

That is a pretty harsh reality to come to terms with, but come to terms with it we must. The buck stops with us and, if we don't look after ourselves, the inevitable will happen: we will get ill or burn out, and the whole house of cards will fall down around us.

It is vital that you prioritise your own needs and make a commitment to mother yourself a bit. Let me make this quite clear: this isn't just something that is nice to do. It is a *necessity*.

If you have children, you will know that the very first time you get sick after you have become a parent is a baptism of fire (as is the very first hangover, but we won't get into that!). I have vivid memories of the first time that I got ill as a new mother. To this day, thirteen years later, I can still remember the horror I felt when I realised that I couldn't just take myself to bed and feel sorry for myself under the covers, watching *Friends* reruns. I *had* to get up, I had to function, and I had to look after a newborn. From that day forward, I vowed that I would make self-care a priority because, when the parent is ill, lots of things have the potential to fall apart. We can't just magically produce a cloned version of ourselves to do the childcare, the cooking, the cleaning and our work!

I come from good stock: a strong, hardy breed of Northern women. If I was a cow, I'd fetch a bloody fortune at the farmers' auction. I have my nana to thank for that; she had the constitution of an ox. She grew up during the Second World War and, back then, self-care wasn't really the buzz word it is today! So, I do understand the urge to just pull up your socks and get on with it. I have to fight it too.

Let's talk about it, because I know that it will resonate with many of you. I can guarantee that there will be a lot of heads nodding along in agreement with this section of the book.

I am a mum to three boys and a step-mum. I have a dog, I run the house, I cook, I clean and I work from home. All of these things are my job. *But I can't call in sick.* I can't pull the duvet over my head and phone my boss to tell them I am not coming in. (Do I even have a boss? ... I suppose you could count Ben, the five-year-old tyrant.)

I have no family who live close by, so if I get ill and can't carry on, it falls to my husband to pick up the slack. I am so thankful to have him around to help. I know from experience how hard it is and how lonely it can feel when you are a single parent who is carrying all of the load. This means Mike has to take time off work and rearrange his units to make sure that the important things get done: you know, like the kids getting fed and making sure that they arrive at school dressed.

If I get ill, it has a butterfly effect on lots of people. Mike's meetings will get cancelled, directly affecting his colleagues and their travel plans. When he gets back to work, he will have a mountain of stuff to catch up on.

What's the answer? Well (apart from the not-very-helpful 'Just don't get sick!'), the short answer is self-care.

Self-care is so important. It might seem like something that is wishy-washy and belongs at the very bottom of your to-do list. If, to you, self-care is something that only exists in the shiny world of social media, where it has its own hashtag and means drinking green smoothies and wearing yoga leggings, then you owe it to yourself to use some of your time for you. You can't keep pushing on forever. There will come a point when you need to take a break.

Remember: when *you* break, *everything* breaks! You mustn't let it get to that point.

Please promise me to plan those level threes with as much care and attention as you would plan your level ones and level twos. Don't leave the level threes to chance, or they will never happen.

RETRAINING YOURSELF TO RELAX

Now this is something I am willing to bet that, back when you were a slip of a girl, you never thought you would one day have to do. You would not have thought that, by the time you were a mum, you would have to *force* yourself to take some time for yourself. Not only that, but that it would feel like such an alien concept after years of putting everyone else's needs before your own, that you would have to retrain your brain just to get it to go into relaxation mode.

When you start to add some decent chunks of relaxation time into your days and weeks, it might start off feeling weird, or a bit like you are rebelling. One of the reasons for this is because you will be planning in your level-three time on a regular basis rather than once in a blue moon. How many of you have *finally* got together with your friends (maybe for one of the most elusive of all level threes – the spa weekend!) only to work out that it has been *months* since you all last saw each other? You sit there, working it out, thinking, 'Nah, that can't be right.' But it is, because life has got in the way and none of you could find the time.

I want that to be a thing of the past.

With TOTT, you will get into the habit of planning in regular level-three time and this will eventually start to become a normal part of your life's structure. It will take practice because you are breaking the habit of self-neglect, but you need to push through that feeling of awkwardness and guilt and trust that planning in your level threes is not only OK but one hundred per cent necessary, for both your mental and physical wellbeing.

HOW TO DEAL WITH SLEEP DEPRIVATION

As a mum of three, I have had my fair share of sleep-deprived stages. The universe decided to throw me a particularly massive curve ball when it gave me my third and final child, who was the worst sleeper in all the world. He didn't sleep through the night until he was *four years old*!

Four. Years. Old.

One morning when he was a baby, I came downstairs to prepare his first bottle of the day and to make myself a much-needed coffee. I was so tired that, in all probability, I was probably not properly awake and simply operating on autopilot.

I put the coffee granules in the bottle. And the formula in the coffee cup.

Luckily, I realised my mistake and corrected it before I gave my four-month-old a bottle of coffee.

If you are suffering from sleep deprivation, here are my top tips to weather the storm.

Get out of the house every day. Get into the fresh air and go somewhere where your kids can let off a bit of steam. Try to head to a playgroup or a park, somewhere where you can talk to another adult who understands what it feels like. I get that it can be really hard to contemplate putting on your make-up and heading out of the door with what is, in all probability, an already fractious child. Your patience will be thin due to you being tired to your bones, but I guarantee that it will help you feel better to get out. You might even be able to talk to someone who is going through the same thing and you can provide each other with a shoulder to cry on. When I was a fourth trimester teacher, I would always

▶

begin my classes with tea and cake for the mums. Before we started, I would make sure that they had time to chat about what had happened the night before and to share tips and support. Never underestimate the power of being able to talk to someone who is willing to listen, and never underestimate the power of being able to talk to someone who you know gets it.

Make sure that you really look after your nutrition. When we are tired, we often reach for quick fixes to keep us going, but these always make us feel worse. Make sure that you eat well and drink enough water. Don't rely on coffees and crisps to get you through the day.

Make sure you get as much sleep as you can. I know, I know! The irony of this statement is not lost on me. But I know that, when you get to the end of the day, the kids have finally settled, and you potentially have a couple of hours to yourself, you want to catch up on the last few episodes of the box set that you have been watching. So, you watch one episode, then another and then another. Before you know it, you are slumped on the sofa, pretending to watch it with one eye open, desperately trying to stay awake because you need to feel like you've had some time to yourself. I know that going to bed earlier can sometimes seem like you are just sleeping and taking care of the kids on a never-ending cycle but, in order to navigate a rocky sleep patch, it is *vital* that you get sleep whenever you can.

Think about using some of your level threes just for sleep. It is temporary; it won't go on forever, and you will feel a lot better for getting an early night. The alternative is having a late night followed by disrupted sleep, which is a recipe for disaster.

Know your limits. Maybe even do a mini temporary time cull and get rid of anything that is proving to be a little too much right now. Again, it is only temporary. You just need to do what is necessary at the moment to make sure that you are looking after yourself just as well as you are looking after your children.

Sleep deprivation is hard work! Never feel bad for making choices that will help you to keep the wheels on your life. Remember: parenting is a marathon, not a sprint – and there certainly isn't a medal for the most tired person at the end of it.

There is no need to prove to yourself, or to anyone else, how busy you are. Your worth is not measured by how much you can squeeze into your day.

9

The Guilt Gremlins

Hands up who feels as though they could do a better job as a mum?

Hands up if you feel guilty getting a babysitter so that you can *finally* get together with your friends, even though this much-needed evening out has been months in the making, as trying to find a night where you were all free was seemingly impossible now that you all have kids?

Hands up who feels as though they do not see their extended family enough?

As you know, I am writing this book during the Covid-19 outbreak and we are all being asked by the government to stay in our homes as much as possible. All pubs and restaurants are closed and the whole country is currently in lockdown, meaning we are housebound. Mike, the kids and I are trying to live our lives as normally as possible, but that's a bit tricky during a lockdown. Mike and I are trying to balance working full-time with making sure the kids' brains don't turn to mush (their school has been closed). So, needs must, and I have taken the whole weekend to get as much of this book done as I can, so that I can rearrange my time units next week to make things more balanced. A few minutes ago, my sister phoned me. We haven't spoken in a few days, but I told her that I would call her back tomorrow because, at this point, time has never been so stretched and I need to use the free units I have this weekend to get this book written. It is my priority, and I know that, once it is finished, I can start to claw back more units to help the kids with their schoolwork. Thank God TOTT is so flexible! But guess what? Yes, you guessed it: after I ended the call, the guilt came rushing in thick and fast.

She'll think you're being funny with her.

She'll be sad now.

You shouldn't have said that you didn't have time to talk. She'll feel undervalued.

In this situation, I had to trust my decision to end the call. We have to make our decisions about how to best use our time based on the information that we have. So, for example, I know that my life will be harder next week if I don't do this now. I know that writing today is the best use of my units. I know that I am doing my utmost in a very tricky situation. I know that my big sis knows that I love her very much, but that right now my work has to come first because I have to pay the bills.

As mums we have to make these decisions (often on the fly) many times a day. And a lot of the time it feels easier to sacrifice our own time so that we can keep the peace and tread the path of least resistance. Often, we do this so that we don't make the people we love feel bad, or simply to avoid inconveniencing the people around us.

The guilt gremlins can come at us from different sources, both in the real world and online. We all have triggers that the guilt gremlins like to press; they enjoy making us feel bad and they just *love* to make us question our choices.

GUILT AND MEMES

Lots of lovely, guilt-ridden memes have popped up on my social media feeds over the years and, oh boy, how some of them have haunted me! This one is by far and away the worst culprit for making me feel as though I am a bad mum and for allowing that insidious, toxic guilt to creep in: 'A good mum has a dirty oven and sticky floors.'

When I have a clean and tidy home, it makes me happier, which means that I am a calmer mum. But according to this meme, I'm not a good mum because I've cleaned the oven and mopped the floors. Memes like this pop up on my feed from time to time, making me feel that the fact that I don't spend all my time building Lego and baking cakes with my kids means that I am a bad mum. These statements can make me think twice about how I prioritise my days, and some can make me feel like I have somehow been falling short as a mum.

We can't win. It seems as though the guilt is always lying in wait. We feel it if our house is too clean. We feel it if our house is not clean enough. We feel it if we go out to work. We feel it if we stay at home. It's enough to make our head spin.

The only thing we can do is work towards making sure that we are making ourselves and our families happy. Everyone else can pipe down. And if they give you trouble, tell them to come and talk to me, and I will sort them out for you!

There is a *massive* subtext bubbling under the surface of memes like this. And that is a subtext of guilt (oh, the irony!). Often, the person posting the meme is trying to ease another exhausted mum's guilt. It might have been intended as a comforting statement for the mum who has been up all night feeding her baby and is too tired to even contemplate getting dressed, let alone scrub the oven (sleep deprivation, anyone?). But by easing one mum's guilt, it can also lump more guilt on to another mum's shoulders.

So why do we feel we need to justify our actions and parenting choices, all the way down to how we choose to spend our time? In short, it is our inherent instinct to be the best parents we can possibly be. But, in all probability, the only one who is judging you is you. I think it's fair to say that most normal people (and we are not talking keyboard warriors or internet trolls here) are too busy trying to live their own lives to worry about criticising the minutiae of how you are running yours. And as for those who do choose to pass comment or judgement: well, maybe they are feeling bad about their choices and are projecting their own guilt on to you.

THE ONSET OF GUILT

Looking after children, running a home and holding down a job is hard work, and this means that sometimes things just won't get done. Or perhaps they will get done, but they'll be a little bit below your usual standards.

Going through the TOTT process might make you feel that pang of guilt coming from more than one direction (oh, joy of joys!) because it might uncover some truths that you have been deliberately avoiding and burying for some time.

The first onset of guilt might come as soon as you have finished Bootcamp, when you might realise how much of your time you had been wasting on things that were not of any benefit to you. Things like, oh, I don't know, scrolling through TikTok? There is nothing you can do about it now, and there is no point in beating yourself up about it. What is done is done. Make your peace with the fact that you can't change the past. You only have the ability to change your actions in the present and in the future. Take a deep breath and let that guilt go. There is absolutely no point in crying over spilled milk.

Do not, I repeat, do *not* worry about it.

The next attack of guilt might come when you start your time cull. I can pretty much guarantee that, when you start making those phone calls, sending those texts and writing those emails to let people know that you might have to renege on something to which you had previously committed, you will start to question if you are doing the right thing. And not only that, you will also start to worry about what people will think of you. I need you to stay strong for this bit. You cannot carry on doing more things than you have the time or the headspace for. You will end up making yourself ill and, when you are out of action, you will be no use to anyone.

Take another deep breath and prioritise yourself and your health (both physical and mental).

And finally, the next bit of guilt could come in when you start to add in your level threes: when you put the car into gear for the first time to head to the gym, or when you run the bath at 8 p.m. instead of sitting down for another evening of trying to catch up on work that you couldn't get done during the day. You might ask yourself if you deserve it. I will answer that question for you. You do. And, in a couple of weeks' time, you will feel much better about sinking down beneath those bubbles – you might have even added in a glass of wine and a good book by then! I promise you, it gets easier.

When the guilt gremlins come a-knocking, I want you to be steadfast in your choices. I want you to trust yourself to make the right decisions: decisions that will make you healthier and happier and, in turn, make life better for those who you love and live with.

It is time to be your own lobster (just wanted to throw in that *Friends* reference ... hey, I love a theme!).

WHAT TO DO WHEN OTHER PEOPLE AREN'T ON THE TOTT TRAIN

What happens when you encounter other people who are not following TOTT?

This is something you will no doubt have to deal with at some point during the TOTT process. We've already talked about how to handle it if your partner isn't onboard (chapter five), but you might find that your workmates or other parents at the school gates start putting in little digs.

'Ooh, off to the gym again, I see. It's all right for some.'

'If only I had the time to go for a nap in the day.'

Repeat after me:

I WILL NOT FEEL GUILTY FOR RUNNING MY DAY LIKE A BOSS.

I WILL NOT FEEL GUILTY FOR RUNNING MY DAY.

I WILL NOT FEEL GUILTY.

This next sentence is going to sound cut-throat and a little bit mean. But stick with me because it is important: sometimes you have to be a little bit cruel to be kind.

If other people don't have the time to do the things you

are now able to enjoy, that is *their* problem. Do not let other people project their problems on to you.

There is no point arranging your day in such a way that you leave yourself enough time to go to the gym four times a week if you just end up feeling guilty the whole time you are there. Deadlifts are nowhere near as much fun when you have a guilt gremlin running around inside your head.

It's normal for other people to feel a bit confused when they see someone who is not only successful, but who also seems to have a fair bit of spare time to boot. It seems to go against the grain. Because you don't seem to be rushing around, they could make the assumption (if they don't implement TOTT) that you just aren't as busy as they are. It isn't their fault that they don't get it. After all, isn't this just how we are told we should be: constantly running around, chasing our tails?

And isn't this exactly what I was worried about when I joined the gym? I was afraid that people would assume that I was shirking my more important responsibilities and just lazing around in a spa all day.

I was worried they'd judge me.

'Who does she think she is?'

'It's all right for her!'

I have been in the public eye for about three years now. Because of this, more people are able to see what I do, and the inevitable outcome is that they will judge me – and some of those judgements will be negative.

In the past when I assessed my time, the only people whose opinion I cared about were those close to me. No one else was able to see how I was running my day. Now, though, my life is very different: I have hundreds of thousands of people following me on my social media channels, and they are all able to see how I run my days. After wrestling with the fact that I didn't want anyone to think that I was lazy, it became clear to me that, unless I spoke up about it, things would never change. Mums and parents would forever feel as though they were in some way being selfish for doing something for themselves.

I decided to put on my big-girl pants and talk about it.

In an Instagram post, I confided in my social media audience, biting the bullet and explaining why I felt as though I deserved to do something for myself. The overwhelmingly positive response was eye-opening. I learned that people had done the same as I had, or had felt inspired to do so, based on my post. Some people explained that seeing someone else doing it and saying it was OK gave them permission to do it, too, without feeling guilty.

I have to say, though, that the guilt did take quite a long time to fully dissipate. I felt so bad that my husband, Mike, didn't have the same outlet for himself that I spent two months persuading him to join the gym too. It was mostly to assuage to my own guilt, but he loves it just as much as I do now.

BE REALISTIC

As young girls, we were sold a utopian vision of adulthood that would allow us to hold down our own careers, have a happy family and pursue our dreams. Now, as adults, we know that our reality is actually quite different. If we are unable to afford help with some of the operational tasks in our life, things like childcare, cleaning, etc., then it will fall to us, as the adults, to complete these tasks. And, as we know, these all take time away from doing the things that make us happy and the things that will push us forward in life. In some cases, these operational tasks will take time away from making money.

You simply can't do all the things. Something has to give. Didn't Bridget Jones say just that?

'It is a truth universally acknowledged that when one part of your life starts going okay, another falls spectacularly into pieces.'
Helen Fielding, novelist

But it shouldn't have to be this way. Part of the solution to this very modern problem is that we have to be realistic when we create the framework of our life. We have to be realistic when we put together our TOTT plan.

We can't expect to work a sixty-hour week and still have time for the gym, putting our kids to bed, training for a tri- athlon, learning a new language, reading one book a week, date nights and weekends away with our friends. We need to prioritise.

A WOMAN'S WORK IS NEVER DONE

Let's finish this chapter by talking briefly about to-do lists. Many of us seem to have a real love for them. Lists are great and they certainly have their place, but if your to-do list is causing you to feel guilty, I want you to try to shift your perspective slightly. I want you to ask yourself the following question:

Will I ever actually be done?

Because – and I'm sorry to be the one to tell you this – the answer to that question is no. The only time your to-do list will ever be truly done is when it is your time to shuffle off this mortal coil.

I am not telling you this to try to depress you. I am telling you this to *free* you. (And, no, I have not lost the plot.)

We need to stop falling into the trap of telling ourselves that we only deserve to rest and relax when we've finished a, b and c. We need to stop forcing ourselves to hustle and grind until we have done x, y and z. Your to-do list is actually never-ending. Have you ever noticed that, as soon as you have finished one job or task, another one usually hops on to the bottom of the list?

That's life.

Stop pushing yourself to do more than you need to, and

stop feeling guilty if you fall short – you are following TOTT now! If you have completed all your units and done everything that you had planned to do today, that is good enough. Tomorrow will come around soon enough, so stop pushing too hard. This is what makes us eat into our level threes, and there's no point: the to-do list never truly gets done.

And that's OK. Tomorrow is another day, and it will bring with it a fresh new batch of level-one and level-two time to start ticking off that list again.

10

Lazy Days

We can all be lazy at times. There should be no shame in admitting that you are having a lazy day. In this book I am trying to actively *encourage* you to plan in some lazy time! It is *unhealthy* for us to be constantly on the go. I know busyness can be worn like a badge of honour, but you will be doing yourself no favours if you do not plan in downtime.

Laziness only really becomes a problem when it starts to become the norm and you find that your lazy days are far outnumbering your productive ones. That is when it can start to infect the rest of your mindset. It can start with one slow afternoon: maybe you put a couple of things off until tomorrow because they are not urgent and you quite fancy leaving work early, only to not get round to doing them the next day either because you still feel a bit 'meh'. If this starts to become regular, you soon find yourself on the fast train to Not-Getting-Much-Doneville, that place where it is much more desirable to binge-watch YouTube videos than do anything productive.

Procrastination and indecisiveness are two of the most common ways that inactivity can stealthily make its way into our lives. But sometimes inactivity makes an appearance out of necessity. When this happens, it can be your body trying to tell you to slow down.

I will give you an example of something that happened to me very recently. I was overdoing it. I was well overdue a Time Bootcamp, but work and life had run away with me and I was trying to fit too much in. I was starting to get tired and stressed out. I was snapping at Mike and the kids and I was feeling really down on myself about the fact that I wasn't coping. So much so that, one day, my brain had had enough. I was so tired that all I could do was stare blankly at the wall. I felt as though my brain could not fit anything in.

It was clearly time for a mini Time Bootcamp. I took the hint that my worn-out mind and body were giving me, and I assessed everything that I had on my plate. I immediately and ruthlessly culled anything that I did not class as essential. And believe me, when I say I was ruthless, I really mean it. Over and over, for each task, I asked myself the killer question: 'What will happen if I don't do it?'

Now don't get me wrong. Sending the emails and making the phone calls to tell people that I was going to have to postpone work, extend deadlines and potentially disappoint them was *not* easy. I felt terrible. But as soon as it was over, the immense weight that had been lifted off my shoulders made it all worth it. It wasn't until that weight was lifted that I realised just how much it had been affecting me. I was like a modern-day equivalent of Marley's ghost, carrying around chains (forged by me taking on far too much) that were slowing me down and making me unproductive.

The same thing happened that always happens when I complete a Time Bootcamp and cull. I suddenly had a new lease of life. I felt happier and calmer. And the cherry on the top? Not only did everyone understand when I explained why I was shifting my schedules, I think it gained me a bit more respect, too!

If you find it hard to motivate yourself to get to the bottom of your to-do list, even if you have time to get the stuff done, you need to ask yourself some searching questions. Are you avoiding a certain task for a reason? Are you overwhelmed by your long, monotonous to-do list and don't know where to start? Or are you just plain exhausted from living life at one thousand miles an hour (like I was)? Could this be your body's way of forcing you to slow down a bit?

One thing is for sure. If your body drops hints for you to slow down and you don't listen, then your body will *make* you slow down. So pay attention to the hints, and take a rest if you need one. Having a lazy day is OK. The key is making sure that you balance it with productivity: when you have a good balance of productivity and rest, you will be on to a winner.

OTHER PEOPLE AND THEIR EXPECTATIONS – BLAME IT ON BEYONCÉ!

Of course, I'm not actually blaming anything on Beyoncé. I'm just referring to the memes and quotes that make us feel really bad about ourselves by pointing out that we all have the same number of hours in a day as Beyoncé. Let's get one thing straight: while it is true that we all have the same twenty-four hours in a day as Bey or Kate Middleton, every single one of us has an entirely different set of circumstances and parameters that we have to work within.

So, while memes like this might have their place (because, on the surface at least, they motivate and inspire), when it really comes down to the nitty-gritty they can sometimes do more than harm than good. They exacerbate our fear of other people's expectations of us, which in turn keeps us running on that never-ending hamster wheel.

Whether this pressure of expectation comes from your boss, your other half or your mum, the effect is the same. It makes us feel that, if we are not busy cramming as much as we possibly can into our twenty-four hours, then we have failed, and are just a bit, well, bone idle.

Only you will know if you are being lazy. Only you will truly know if you are using your units as you intended. This whole technique relies on you being accountable to yourself. TOTT relies on you looking at your week with a bird's-eye view and seeing the clear areas of time that you have blocked out in which to be unashamedly lazy. And you should revel in that time, because you will have earned it and it will be guilt-free.

I find that it is much less tempting to have a 'meh' lazy morning when you know that you have a delicious couple of hours coming up later in the week that will be your idea of downtime heaven. This could be a shopping trip, brunch with a friend or even a nap.

Nothing will motivate you to stick to your plan more than that.

If you know that you are prone to more than your fair share of CBA days (Can't Be Arsed days – those of you who have read my first book will know all about these), make sure that you plan in some cracking level-three activities that will spur you on to get everything else out of the way so you can enjoy your level threes wholeheartedly.

In case you haven't realised it yet, *spendthrifts, I am looking directly at you*! How you spend your free time is important; you have to make sure it is truly quality time. It can be all too easy to fall into the trap of wasting precious time, meaning you never really get quality 'me time'. That just leaves you craving more, and so the cycle continues.

A good level-three session has the power to be a fantastic carrot for you. It will help you to compartmentalise the fun from the other daily stuff and you will start to feel as though you are living, rather than just going through the motions.

11

Starting a New Project

I've talked a lot so far about the importance of using the new level-three time in your life for things like self-care and relaxation. But it can also be used to embark on a new project or business venture; and following a passion can be just as invigorating as making time for a long, hot bath or a visit to the gym (spa!).

You might be thinking that spending an hour or so a day on a new project simply isn't enough time to get it off the ground. This is where I show you that that's wrong. So much can be achieved during your level-three time; it just requires a different mindset.

Dreamers, this is your chapter: it's your time to shine! If you are a classic dreamer, you will no doubt have lofty ambitions for the future. Your downfall? Often you get so

blinded by the overwhelming gap between where you currently are and where you want to be that you feel as though
you need to wait for the perfect time before you can start
to work on making that dream a reality. To the typical
dreamer, spending a bit of time working on a goal here and
there will seem like just a drop in the ocean, so they don't
bother. In fact, any step towards a goal is worth taking – no
matter how small.

ALL THOSE LITTLE BITS ADD UP

Every January, I give my social media audience a pep talk
that involves a roll of kitchen towel. It is a treat for the eyes,
I can tell you. But why January – and why kitchen towel?
Quite simply, January is the time of year when people are
going for their goals with all guns blazing, with their New
Year's resolutions locked and loaded in their minds. As for the
kitchen towel: I can't remember who originally came up with
this analogy (hats off to whoever it was!), but it is perfect for
helping us understand how those little bits of effort add up.

Most people start off full of determination, ready to rush
headlong into the first month of the year at one hundred miles
an hour. Then they hit a bump in the road – usually around
mid-January – and, inevitably, find that they are unable to
keep up their break-neck speed for twelve months as they
already feel burned out. They lose motivation and soon they
stop altogether, feeling demotivated and flat.

This of course, can apply to anything, such as a new healthy eating regime or embarking on the Couch-to-5k challenge. For the purposes for this book and for TOTT, we are going to focus on the idea of starting a new project. In particular, we're going to talk about how to deal with that feeling of overwhelm that is so common at the start of a new project, and which can ultimately stop you from achieving your goals.

It can be tempting to put off starting a project until the 'time is right': until you have got all of your ducks in a row and you have enough time to concentrate purely on your new project and that alone. Sometimes we have got so much other stuff going on in our lives that we feel as though we cannot give our project the attention that it might deserve.

If you're reading this book, you are probably time-poor, but with a head full of ambitions (big or small) that you think you will never get the chance to pursue because, quite simply, there just aren't enough hours in the day.

It could be that you really want to write a book (hey, there's one in each and every one of us, apparently).

Maybe you are trying to find the time to set up a side business.

Maybe you want to finally get around to learning to play the flute.

But if you were thinking that you need to wait for the 'perfect time' – what if there is never going to be a 'perfect time'? What if the only time is now?

Many of us, in order to try to fulfil our goals and dreams,

have to try to *find* the time. And we all know that, just as there is no magic money tree, there is also no magic time tree. If we want to fit time for something new into our life, we have to take that time away from something else.

That is why TOTT is so effective. That is why the Bootcamp and the cull are absolutely non-negotiable in this process, because they will help you to work out which things in your life you can *stop* doing so that you can finally fit in the things that you really want to do. Even if that is just reading a chapter of a book each night before you go to sleep.

TOTT doesn't only help you to work out the things you want to prioritise and do in life; it also helps you put some structure in place so that you are able to actually do those things.

But what happens when you are using your level threes to finally get around to starting a project that you have been putting off for years because you never thought you had the time? What happens if, due to the way your life is structured, you never seem to get anywhere? Maybe you have a toddler running around your ankles while you're trying to get your business off the ground?

If you are only working with small chunks of time that you are able to snatch here and there, I have some really good news for you. And yes, you've guessed it, it involves that kitchen roll. In January, when it is time for my New Year's team talk, I always reach for the roll of kitchen towel. Humour me, and let's visualise this together.

Think of one of those mega-bumper rolls of kitchen towel.

Close your eyes and see it. And now imagine tearing one piece off every day. Just one piece daily, no more.

For the first few days, and maybe even for the first couple of weeks, you probably won't notice any difference in the way that the kitchen roll looks. But a few weeks in, if you are diligent about tearing off a piece every day, you will start to see that a real difference has been made in the thickness of that kitchen roll.

This is where the magic starts to happen. This is where all those little bits of time add up. That difference in the thickness of the kitchen roll would not have happened if you had not spent the small amount of time each day taking one piece off. And while, at the time, it would have looked as though it had had no effect, suddenly, thirty days later, the cumulative effect is visible.

When you apply this to time, you can see how thirty minutes a day (or even less) can all add up towards a greater goal. Maybe it's taking thirty minutes a day to write 500 words for a book: in two months, you will have written 30,000 words. Maybe it's spending thirty minutes a day doing marketing calls or emails. Maybe it's spending thirty minutes a day tackling the major declutter-thon that is the garage.

All these chunks of units will add up.

So, to all the dreamers and planners out there who feel overwhelmed at the thought of starting a project that just seems too high a mountain to climb with the small amount of daily time that you have available, take heart.

It doesn't matter how fast you achieve your goals, as long as you are moving forwards and making progress. Whether it's one page of your book or one mile completed in your training for your first marathon, all of those little bits will add up.

GEM'S TOP TIP

Instead of concentrating on the end goal, which in some cases can be extremely daunting, turn your concentration to what it is you need to do on a daily, weekly or monthly basis to actually get it done.

For example, let's say that you have decided to fulfil an ambition and have signed up for your first half marathon. The thought of having to run twenty-one kilometres terrifies you: the nearest you have ever got to a race until now is your local park run on a Saturday morning. It can be so daunting that you just don't know where to start. So, in the end, it just seems easier not to. Those trainers never do the miles and you never see race day.

Don't give in to stage fright. Instead, break the training down into smaller, more manageable (and less scary) chunks, and focus on those little goals rather than the big end one. By working out how many miles you need to run each week, and how much you need to increase your mileage on a weekly basis, you will shift your concentration away from the Big Race to smaller, innocent runs around your local area.

Trusting in the compounding effect of your smaller efforts will take the feeling of overwhelm away from the end goal. The end goal will, in fact, be taking care of itself in the background without you even having to put too much thought into it, because you have now shifted your concentration on to doing the smaller tasks that are needed to get the bigger task done.

Whether it is training for a half marathon, writing a book or starting a new business, all of the little bits of effort *will* add up. One day you will look back and see just how far forward those little steps have moved you towards your goal.

12

Using TOTT in the Workplace

Do you feel frazzled at work? Do you dream of being able to fly through your in tray like some sort of administrative ninja? Do you fantasise about batting off unnecessary meeting requests to preserve that sacred lunchtime as the jewel in the crown of your working day?

You're in the right place.

You might think that TOTT is only applicable to your life outside work and be tempted to view the time you allocate to work as one big chunk that you can't break down in the same way. But the glorious beauty of TOTT is that you can assign your units to whatever you want. The technique is just as effective in helping you work out how you are going to bring order back to your working life as it is in your home life, from fitting in a long bubble bath every Sunday night to making sure that, when you log off at work on a Friday, you have completed all of your assigned tasks for the working week.

Putting your units to work in the workplace will not only bring order to what might be inbox chaos, it will also help you to be much less stressed and, in turn, make you more productive, meaning you are much more likely to get that promotion (winning!).

With that in the back of our minds, spurring us on, let's get cracking and see how powerful those little units can be in your nine-to-five.

Now obviously, each and every one of us is going to have a different working day (because we all do different jobs). Some of you will work part-time, others will do more than one job, others won't work in an office at all and some of you will work from home, but the basic principles of TOTT can be applied to most jobs that allow you to structure your own day.

WORKING OUT UNITS AT WORK

For the purposes of our example we are going to look at an office worker, let's call her Sarah. Sarah works five days a week as an administrator for an estate agency and her working hours are 9 a.m. to 5 p.m. Pretty standard so far. That means that she is in work for 8 hours each day (16 units). She takes an hour for lunch (2 units), which leaves her with 14 units.

Her main duties are checking and replying to emails, maintaining the company website (updating listings) and booking in viewings for the sales team. At the moment, she feels as though her days are a bit of a muddle. She often feels as though she is being reactive at work rather than in control, so let's try to bring a bit of order to her day.

When she gets into work in the morning there are always lots of messages waiting. Customers have sent in enquiries about properties via email and voice message overnight. It makes sense to assign some of Sarah's units at the very start of the working day to going through these. Let's assign 1 hour to this (2 units).

This leaves her with 12 units.

During the morning, Sarah is expected to help answer the phones and do operational tasks to support the sales team. Let's assign 2 hours to this, which she can keep free, allowing her to be reactive without feeling as though she is being taken away from another task. That has taken up 4 units.

This leaves her with 8 units.

This brings her nicely up to lunch (for which we have already assigned 2 units).

Sarah is working on giving the company website an overhaul, as it was looking a bit old-fashioned and out of date, but she needs to concentrate on this task as it is complicated. The office is generally much quieter in the afternoon as her colleagues are usually out at viewings. It therefore makes sense to assign 2 hours to this task in the afternoon (taking up 4 units).

This leaves her with 4 units.

Sarah then assigns another 2 units to helping with any operational tasks that the team need assistance with over the course of the afternoon.

Leaving her with 2 units.

She leaves these 2 units till the end of the day as a contingency or catch-all to make sure she can help out with any unforeseen little jobs that might crop up. If they go unused, then she can use them to do some general admin tasks that might have been languishing on the to-do list for a while.

We can see how easily the TOTT plan is applied to a typical working day, but it can also be applied just as easily if you work from home. I know how easy it is, because I use TOTT on every single one of my working days. Granted, things are looking a little different for me at the moment due to Covid-19, but I am going to show you how I structured my working day (as a blogger and writer) before.

My working day would consist of 8.5 hours (17 units).

9.30–10.30 a.m. – Reply to emails and social media comments (2 units).

10.30–11.30 a.m. – Operational tasks, such as accounts/marketing/phone meetings/editing (2 units).

11.30 a.m.–12.30 p.m. – Plan social media posts (2 units).

12.30–1.30 p.m. – Lunch (2 units).

1.30–3.30 p.m. – Creative projects (such as writing/filming YouTube videos/recording podcast) (4 units).

3.30–4.30 p.m. – Gym (2 units).

4.30–6 p.m. – Reply to emails and social media comments (3 units).

Now that we are in lockdown, Mike and I are both working from home and we are also supporting the kids with their schoolwork. It means that my time is pressed in a way that it has never been before.

I had to have a mini cull at the start of last week to address this. Below is how I reshuffled my day to make way for the massive impact that Covid-19 has had on my working life. This is the perfect example to show you just how flexible TOTT is and how, if used properly, it can help you through even the trickiest of situations.

Most of our living area downstairs is open-plan and Mike and I don't have any office space, so we all work around the kitchen table. This can be *interesting* but, as I said earlier in the book, we all have to work with what we have. So, this is how we are managing our time right now.

9.30–10.30 a.m. – Reply to emails and social media comments (2 units).
The boys do an online PE session for part of this time. For the other half-hour, they have their breakfast.

10.30–11.30 a.m. – Operational tasks, such as accounts/ marketing/editing (2 units).
Settle the boys in for their homework. I do not need to concentrate too much for these tasks so can help with

homework if needed. I have moved phone meetings to later in the day.

11.30 a.m.–12.30 p.m. – Plan social media posts (2 units).
Boys continue with homework and school activities.

12.30–1.30 p.m. – Lunch (2 units).
We all eat lunch together to keep it simple and keep clean-up to a minimum.

1.30–3.30 p.m. – Creative projects (such as writing/filming YouTube videos/recording podcast) (4 units).
This is the time where I need as much peace and quiet as possible, so the boys get some free time (which usually means they head straight to their screens/Skype their friends).

3.30–4.30 p.m. – *The gym is closed so I do a workout in the garden if the weather is OK, while the boys play outside too. If it is rainy, I work out in the hall and the boys watch TV* (2 units).

4.30–6 p.m. – Phone calls (3 units).
I have reduced the amount of time I usually spend replying to social media and emails to enable me to fit in any phone meetings I need to have. Mike is on hand to keep the boys entertained during this time.

GEM'S THREE GOLDEN RULES FOR STAYING FOCUSED AT WORK

1. Try to schedule your work around when you feel at your most productive

You might be a morning person and get to work bright-eyed and bushy-tailed, ready to kick your to-do list into touch. If this is you, it makes sense to plan the most difficult tasks (i.e. the ones that require the most brain power) for earlier in the day, leaving the more basic, operational tasks for after lunch when you might get the inevitable post-lunch slump. Of course, if you are the other way around and it takes you a couple of hours (and a couple of coffees) to warm up, or if you've just come back to work after maternity leave, and you are still battling with sleepless nights, just do a bit of a switcheroo and schedule your trickier tasks for later in the day, when you're feeling more focused.

2. Stop task jumping

It is absolutely crucial that you focus on one task at a time as much as possible. Try not to let yourself become distracted, otherwise you could be halfway through and fully focused when suddenly your attention is switched to something else. All this will achieve is lots of half-completed tasks that are going to leave you feeling as though you are not making progress. Before you sit down to do a task, make sure that you have enough time to complete it and that you are in the right frame of mind to get it done effectively. You need to guard against task hopping, because this actually wastes time.

3. When you are working on a complicated task, make sure that you turn off your notifications

Turning off notifications and distractions can allow you to fully immerse yourself in your work. Tell people that you won't be around for that time, block out your diary and decline meeting requests. It will save you time and it will earn you the respect of your colleagues.

HOW TO STAY FOCUSED WHEN YOU WORK FROM HOME

I have been working from home for years now and I like to think that I am a bit of a pro at making sure that I get everything done without spending hours on YouTube. Here are my top tips for making sure you stay as focused as possible when your office is the kitchen table.

Pick a concentration playlist

I have a 'concentration playlist' on my Spotify channel that is just under one hour long (two units). I find it is the perfect length to help me bash through a good chunk of work, and it really helps me to focus. I have been listening to the same playlist since I wrote my first book. That's over eighteen months ago now. This means that my brain is now trained. As soon as I hear the first song play (the theme from *Forrest Gump*, if anyone is interested), my brain immediately goes into work mode. It really helps me to power through, especially on days when I feel a bit below par.

As an extension to the above tip, I find that I can't hold that level of focus for more than two units at a time, so I always work in two-unit chunks. You can't expect yourself to keep going non-stop all day. You have to factor in breaks. If you worked in an office, you wouldn't sit at your desk for the full eight hours: you would get up, grab a coffee, go over and talk to a colleague. So, as much as you can, try to plan in similar breaks at home. Maybe walk to a nearby coffee shop to grab a takeaway latte, or go and have a cup of tea in your garden.

Observe your working hours

You need to make sure that you are not distracted from your work as much as possible during your working hours. Truth be told, my parents struggled with this at first. Neither of them had ever worked from home, so they used to find it very hard to understand that although I was at home, I was still at work, and that meant I couldn't pop over during the working day or take random phone calls to talk about nothing in particular. All this has to wait until out-of-work hours, just as it would if you worked in an office.

Get a comfy chair!

This might sound silly and obvious, but if you are not comfy, you will not be able to get into your groove and you won't be as productive as you want to be.

Make sure that you have a lunch break

This is something that I started doing again after a recent Time Bootcamp. I had been getting busier and busier, and this meant that I was working during the time in which I had planned to eat my lunch. Not only was I was working through my lunch break, work was also creeping into other parts of my day, despite my plans. So, I made sure I blocked out my lunch and I have been making myself take that time out. Taking a break helps to keep my mind fresh and helps me to be more focused in the afternoon.

Remember to stop

As an addition to the point above, make sure that you stop your working day at a reasonable time if you can. And, if you do have to work in the evenings (for example, if you have to wait until your toddler is asleep), make sure you structure your TOTT plan accordingly so that you are still getting your level-three time in somewhere.

Plan your day around when you are most productive

I know I already covered this in my golden rules above, but this is really important. I am at my most creative just after lunchtime, so this is usually when I try to sit down and write. I plan the rest of my day around this, but I always make sure that I prioritise the tasks that are going to earn me the most money when I am at my most productive.

13

TeamTOMM's Time-Saving Tips

I hope that you are enjoying following your own TOTT and reaping the benefits that the system brings: more time for yourself; keeping on top of all your essential jobs without feeling frazzled; never feeling like your time is being wasted or passing you by without really having a handle on how you've spent it. However well it's working for you, there are always more ideas you can introduce to help you spend your time even more wisely. So, in this final chapter, I've included some of my top tips for freeing up your time. I've also asked the members of my TOMM online community for their time-saving tips. I hope these will help you take your TOTT plan to the next level!

GEMMA'S TOP TIPS FOR LIGHTENING THE LOAD AND FREEING UP HEADSPACE

Without a doubt, life is getting busier. The sweet irony of it all is that the more time-saving devices we use and buy, the more we end up doing. We *think* it will save us more time in which to do other stuff, so we buy an Alexa, or we buy a tablet so that we can check our emails and read work documents more easily on the train . . . and on it goes! But all that is really happening is we are overfilling our to-do lists (and headspace), which in turn cranks up the stress and ultimately eats into our level-three time.

Here are my top tips to help you find more breathing space in that hectic brain of yours.

Work smarter, not harder

This is such a biggie for me. Efficiency is the key to making less work for yourself. To save yourself from running around like a blue-arsed fly, think smart when devising your TOTT plan. Are there any jobs that you can double up on? Can you phone your mum while walking the dog? Clean the bathroom while the kids are having their bath? Do your pelvic floor exercises while waiting for the traffic lights to turn green? (Hey, don't judge! I've had three kids!)

Learn not to sweat the small stuff

Now, this is certainly something that does *not* come naturally to me. If left unchecked, I will micromanage lots of different elements of my day and it always leaves me frazzled. I have learned to delegate and just breathe when things are not done in *exactly* the way I want. A great example of this is the way I have taught my older kids to make their beds. I tried to teach them how to tuck it all in tightly, but it soon became clear that it wasn't going to happen! I taught them an in-between way that makes my life so much easier. They straighten their bottom sheet, plump up the pillow and fold the duvet in half back over itself. *Et voila*! Not only a neat and tidy bed, but one that will air throughout the day, too! That's one job ticked off the list without me having to lift a finger.

Realise that there are only twenty-four hours in a day

In this book we are learning how important it is to be realistic about what you are going to be able to achieve in the time that one day gives you. If you are working, coming home to kids/homework/dinner/dishes, and wanting to go for a run *and* clean your house *and* catch up with *Big Little Lies*, it won't be long before you run and hide under the bed with brain overload.

If you don't want to do something ... don't do it

This is one of the most freeing things you can allow yourself to do. Just to be clear, I don't mean don't clean the bathroom ... that is an important part of adulting that nobody ever *really* wants to do, and I'm afraid it has to be done! I mean, if you don't want to sign up to be on the PTA, don't feel pressured into doing so. If someone is standing in front of you with a clipboard and you feel pressured to say yes, take a deep breath and say you'll think about it. And then send a very polite but firm email saying you are too busy right now. Seriously, try it – it is *so* bloody liberating! *Start to become the guardian of your own time.*

Learn to let go

In order to simplify your life, you need to start with your mind. I think we are all bombarded with perfection on a minute-by-minute basis. If you have a social media account you will, without a doubt, have been subjected (probably sub-consciously) to lots of images of perfection that might have left you feeling a bit lacking. Let go of that urge to strive for the picture-perfect life and embrace the good enough. Remember the golden rule of TeamTOMM:

GOOD ENOUGH IS GOOD ENOUGH!

TIME-SAVING TIPS FROM THE TOMM COMMUNITY

To end the book, I can think of nothing more fitting than leaving you with some of the top time-saving tips from the hive mind that is TeamTOMM. If you are not a member of the TeamTOMM community, make sure you put that right! Head over to Facebook, search for TeamTOMM and you will find us – as well as lots of hints, tips and support to get your life running like clockwork.

Thank you to everyone who helped to put this section of the book together; you are all superstars!

'I remember that each little step is a goal achieved towards the bigger goal.'
Kirsty

'To save time, I hang my socks in pairs by their toes. When they are dry, it is easy to fold them together before removing from the washing line.'
Rebecca

'I make sandwiches for the next day while I'm
making the dinner. I'm in the kitchen anyway,
waiting for stuff to boil, so it fills the time.'
Emma

'Scan all your important documents, such as pass-
port details, birth certificates, HMRC details,
etc., and put them into a file, so they are easy to
find when you need them!'
Carolyn

'We've got a small five-drawer unit for each child to
organise and store their full, clean school uniform
in for every day of the week. That way we're not
scrambling around for socks or their tie five minutes before heading out the door in the morning!'
Lottie

'When it's time to change the brush head on
your electric toothbrush, use the old one to clean
around your taps, plugholes and anywhere else
tricky to deal with.'
Jen

'I use the time it takes to boil the kettle to do a job in the kitchen: the little bit of washing-up that needs to be done, wiping down the sides, putting away the dishes or cleaning the sink and draining board. It only takes a couple of minutes, and you get a cuppa as a reward.'

Nicole

'When my shopping is delivered, if any of the meals I have planned for the week involve chopping, I do that straight away and then bag up the ingredients together. It saves time on the day you're cooking them, and any extra can be bagged up and frozen for quick use another time. It also saves more fridge and freezer space as they are chopped up and can be stored flat.'

Franchesca

'I keep the kids' activity stuff in separate rucksacks on coat hooks on the back of the doors of their rooms: a Brownies bag, a ballet bag, a swimming bag, etc. Everything is always in the bag and never in a drawer, so it's always ready to grab and go. It means needing a few spare mini hairbrushes, etc., but I found we actually had enough without buying things specially.'

Lucy

'My morning routine, when done daily in the same
order, becomes like a dance. You rehearse the
steps for long enough, and soon you don't even
have to think about it.'
Victoria

'If you have lots of plastic tubs, use a permanent
marker to label the tub and matching lid so that
you can easily match them up, e.g. A tub to A lid,
B tub to B lid.'
Faye

'I have an alarm on my phone in the evening to
remind me to ... put down my phone.'
Louise

I told my kids all the smoke alarms are Santa's
cameras, all year round, and that the flash is
when he takes a photo. If they skip bed-making or
chores, those pictures of unmade beds and messy
rooms, etc. get put on their file! They make their
beds every day now.'
Kelly

'I only check emails after I've cleared a few important items off my own to-do list. Emails usually create work for you, but they're generally for other people's goals, not your own.'
Debs

'Always! Listen! To Gemma! Don't go rogue!!'
Abigail

Conclusion

I hope that you have enjoyed reading this book and that The Organised Time Technique will help you just as much as it has helped me.

At the height of my cleaning obsession, I would spend hours cleaning. I would even cancel social appointments if I thought I hadn't cleaned enough. My self-care dropped to the bottom of the list. I put myself last, after absolutely everything, even after the vacuuming.

This is something that I see play out daily. Women contact me, desperately trying to find a solution. They are exhausting themselves trying to be everything to everyone, and they reach out to me (a stranger on the internet) and take a punt on a system that I created when I was in their position. I lost myself in among the housekeeping, the school runs, the work (both paid and unpaid) and the rest of the life admin that just had to get done. This is an all-too familiar tale for many of us. As women, we often only turn to our own needs once everyone else's needs are taken care of.

It is my mission to help as many mums as I can to find balance – and, not only that, but to find themselves again. If you are already following The Organised Mum Method, you will hopefully have found that balance with the housework. After you implement The Organised Time Technique, that feeling of balance will move into the rest of your life.

I don't want you wasting precious headspace thinking about cleaning and all of the other boring stuff that is getting in the way of you actually *living* your life. I want you to be planning adventures, projects, passions and pursuits.

I hope that this book has helped you to put systems in place so that you don't have to think about the boring stuff for a minute longer than is absolutely necessary. And I hope that it helps you to delegate, so the burden of running your home doesn't fall solely at your feet.

But above all, I hope that it helps you to live the life you dreamed of back when you were a little girl.

Relax, breathe; you've got this.

Lots of love,

Gem

Acknowledgements

To the TOMM community, thank you for your shares, likes, comments and all-round fabulousness! Your support means the world. And what would that community be without our fantastic team of moderators? You ensure the mammoth Facebook group is a great place to share hints, tips and support. Thank you for giving up your time to help keep it that way.

To my husband Mike, thank you for being my Colonel Brandon and for all the cups of tea (I promise to put the kettle on more).

To my beautiful boys, Tom, Jonny and Ben, I love you all the world (ten times over!). Thank you for being the best kids a mum could wish for.

To my mum, dad and big sister, thank you for all your love and support (and for buying all the newspapers and magazines I have been in!).

To Chippy, I am thankful daily that the crazy world of Instagram threw us together.

To Zoe, thank you for being the best PA in the world ever, bar none!

And *of course* a massive shout-out to the amazing team at Piatkus and Little, Brown. I could not have wished for a more supportive and patient bunch. Thank you.

Index